THE
# MODERN
# DOG PARENT
HANDBOOK

Copyright © 2023 Bryce and Kenzie Francois

First published in 2023 by
Page Street Publishing Co.
27 Congress Street, Suite 1511
Salem, MA 01970
www.pagestreetpublishing.com

Distributed by Macmillan, sales in Canada by The Canadian Manda Group.

27   26   25   24   23      1   2   3   4   5

ISBN-13: 978-1-64567-918-9
ISBN-10: 1-64567-918-7

Library of Congress Control Number:  2022952257

Cover and book design by Meg Baskis for Page Street Publishing Co.
Photography by Laurel Place

Printed and bound in China

# THE
# MODERN
# DOG PARENT
# HANDBOOK

The Holistic Approach to Raw Feeding, Mental Enrichment
and Keeping Your Dog Happy and Healthy

BRYCE AND
KENZIE FRANCOIS
Creators of The BK Pets

PAGE STREET
PUBLISHING CO.

# CONTENTS

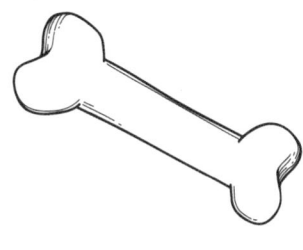

## DISCLAIMER

Please note that throughout this book, you may come across information that conflicts with your current approach to caring for your dog. This is not intended to shame or criticize you, but simply to provide new information you may not have been aware of before. We understand everyone starts somewhere, and the fact that you are reading this book shows you are willing to learn and improve your dog's health and well-being. We are proud of you for taking this step and are honored to be a part of your journey.

The information provided in this book is not intended to replace the advice of a veterinarian. It is only intended to provide general information on caring for your dog's health and well-being. If you have any specific questions or concerns about your dog's health, please consult a veterinarian immediately. We cannot be held liable for any actions taken or not taken based on the information provided in this book.

# FOREWORD

In *De Alimento*, a text written by Hippocrates, there is a statement that reads, "In food excellent medicine can be found, in food bad medicine can be found; good and bad are relative." This could also be interpreted as: Some foods can cure disease, and other foods can cause more illness. This statement certainly applies to the food we feed our dogs.

For decades, the veterinary profession has colluded with large pet food manufacturers to encourage parents to feed their pets highly processed foods devoid of high-quality, human-grade ingredients. "Prescription diets" routinely prescribed by veterinarians are meant to cure and prevent disease, duping unsuspecting pet parents into believing these diets have medicinal properties. If these diets are believed to be so effective, why are we seeing more chronic inflammatory diseases, allergies, endocrine disease and cancer in dogs? In reality, when dogs are fed real food, whole foods and human-grade foods, the transition from disease to good health can be nothing short of miraculous.

Unfortunately, as explained by Bryce and Kenzie throughout this book, most veterinarians have minimal training in diet formulation. They believe the myths that dogs must be fed the same processed food every day for life and that every meal must be complete and balanced to achieve good health. Until the veterinarians see the value in feeding fresh food nutrition to dogs, they will remain steadfast in their beliefs. Many times, it is up to the pet parent to take the bull by the horns and make changes toward a better diet to improve the health of their dog.

This book helps owners feel empowered to start making changes in the bowl that improve health and longevity. Meal boosters and supplements are a great way to start small, as they test to see whether a dog has preferences for certain foods while building confidence to move on to completely home-prepared meals. For those who despise math, Bryce and Kenzie have done the work for you!

Veterinarians who do not feel comfortable designing diets for their patients can use this book as a guide to help pet parents get started. While there are many people who will shun fresh feeding, opting for processed, "complete and balanced" foods, I believe the push by loving pet owners opting for better nutrition will eventually win them over.

—Dr. Judy Morgan, DVM, CVA, CVCP, CVFT

*Judy Morgan*

# INTRODUCTION

We're Bryce and Kenzie Francois, a married couple from Wyoming with a love so deep for animals, we decided to dedicate our entire lives to helping them live as long as possible. We met during a social media internship with the University of Wyoming Athletics Department. After meeting, we instantly hit it off and became great friends and coworkers. We were always making content together, creating videos together and inevitably started dating in 2017.

Over the next few years, we acquired our three dogs: Harper, Cooper and Banksy. Harper and Cooper are Australian Shepherd siblings with the same parents but from different litters. Banksy is a rescue that came to us from the freezing temperatures and blackouts that Texas experienced back in 2021. He is a mixed breed, but his DNA testing kit says he is mostly Husky, though you wouldn't be able to tell just by looking at him!

In 2021, we began transitioning our dogs to a raw/gently cooked diet after listening to a few podcasts with Dr. Karen Becker and Rodney Habib (whom we talk about later). They were talking about dogs and evolution—specifically, how dogs have evolved over millions of years to eat a raw diet, and that kibble has only been fed to them for about the last 100 years. This got us thinking and questioning why highly processed food pellets are the most common food being pushed for our furry family members. We began sharing our journey with the community we built from our business, about 200k people on TikTok at the time. As of writing this in December 2022, we have a community of over 1.5 million pet parents who trust us to provide them with the correct information in hopes of getting as many years with their beloved animals as possible. We couldn't be more grateful for the support of our community and for you being here today, reading this book.

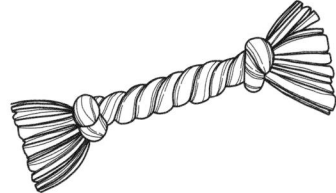

We understand that not everyone may already be familiar with the concepts or techniques outlined in this book, and we don't want to shame or criticize those who are not currently feeding a fresh diet to their pets. Everyone has to start somewhere, and we want to provide the necessary information and resources to empower pet parents to make healthier choices for their beloved animals. Just a few years ago, we were also feeding our dogs kibble, which we believe was at the root of many ailments our dogs experienced, and it wasn't until we learned more that we were able to make the switch to a homemade diet.

Our goal with this book is to help others feel confident in their ability to do the same, just as they would when preparing meals for themselves and their families. If you don't feel like you have the time or resources to feed a fully homemade diet, we have an entire chapter on improving the food you currently feed your dog, regardless of what it is. You'll also learn how to shop for dog food and what ingredients to look out for, how to decrease boredom behaviors, and how to provide mental stimulation to keep your dog's mind younger, longer—and so much more that we can't wait for you to read. We truly believe this book will be a long-term resource you will utilize on your path to enriching and extending the lives of your companions.

One theme you'll notice throughout this book is that, for the most part, we don't give specific product recommendations. This is because businesses and their products change so often that it would be almost impossible to keep this book up-to-date. Instead, we list all of our favorite products on our website, thebkpets.com, as well as on our social media channels, @thebkpets.

Again, thank you so much for being here today, and let's get started helping your dog live the longest, healthiest life they can.

*Kenzie Francois*

# Part One

# EXTENDING YOUR DOG'S LIFE

Chapter 1

# THE HISTORY OF BIG KIBBLE AND HOW IT'S MADE

## THE HISTORY OF KIBBLE

Dogs have been a companion to humans for the last 30,000-plus years. Up until about 200 years ago, their diet consisted of the same foods as ours, including meat, fruits and vegetables, bread and other grains, as well as wild game that they hunted. In the late 1800s, an electrician named James Spratt saw some stray dogs eating hardtack. Hardtack was a dry, hard cracker or bread-like food made from flour, water and sometimes salt. It was very popular among sailors because it wouldn't spoil and it helped curb their hunger on long ventures. Spratt decided to try and make his own version of hardtack for dogs because he saw a huge gap in the market that he could potentially fill, while simultaneously filling his own pockets with money. Thus, Spratt's Dog and Puppy Cakes were born. His version was made from flour, beef blood, beetroot, various vegetables and mystery meat of unknown origin.

Hardtack was not very nutritious and was difficult to eat, but this didn't stop Spratt from pricing his new formula at an average person's daily salary for one 50-pound (22.7-kg) bag. He knew the average person wouldn't be willing or able to pay this much, so he decided to try and convince the wealthiest of Americans that his food was superior. At the time, this happened to be upper-class hunters and their hunting dogs. Once he was able to convince them, he was ready to target the average health-conscious pet owners. Spratt began aggressively marketing his biscuits and even took out a front-page ad in the very first *American Kennel Club Journal*.

As time went on, he wasn't quite done with the upper-class hunting community and called upon them to write raving reviews about his product and the benefits that came from it. He called on these people specifically because of their wealth and influence. It only took a few years for his marketing strategy to work, and ultimately most of the nation's pet owners began feeding his highly processed, not very nutritious cakes to their pets instead of the fresh food scraps and homemade meals they used to feed them.

Competitors began to emerge and new products started hitting the shelves, bringing canned dog food into the picture. In the 1920s, Ken-L Ration was one of the leaders in canned pet food, offering recipes with "lean red meat." It was horse meat. During this time, hundreds of thousands of horses were being bred and slaughtered just for dog food every single year. When World War II broke out, metal was in high demand and dog food was deemed nonessential, so pet food companies had to shift to a product that more closely resembled Spratt's original creation—essentially dry dog food. General Mills ended up acquiring Spratt's business, and they began making dog food using the same exact process they used to make their cereal (more on extrusion later). From there, Ralston Purina was born.

# HOW KIBBLE IS MADE AND WHY IT'S PROBLEMATIC

We now know the backstory, so how exactly is kibble made? The Global Alliance of Pet Food Associations (GAPFA) states, "Dry pet foods are made by mixing dry and wet ingredients together to form a dough. In the extrusion process, the dough is heated under pressure, then pushed through a die machine that cuts the kibbles. Kibble size and shape vary according to the product specification. The kibbles are dried, cooled and spray coated. Some dry foods may also be produced by means other than extrusion, such as baking." Seems pretty straightforward, right? Actually, there's a lot more to it, so let's break down each sentence of the GAPFA statement and talk about what exactly it means.

"Dry pet foods are made by mixing dry and wet ingredients together to form a dough." What are these wet and dry ingredients they speak of? One of the most unsavory ones could be what is called 4D meat (dead, diseased, dying, disabled), which is meat from an animal that did not die via slaughter. Commonly, these meats are sprayed with denaturing chemicals to ensure they leave the human supply chain. These chemicals can be really harsh, such as creosote. According to Dr. Conor Brady in his book *Feeding Dogs: Dry or Raw? The Science Behind the Debate*, "This denaturing involves covering the meat with any number of toxic substances, creosote being a particularly nasty one. A tar-oil derivative, creosote was until recently used as a disinfectant or to preserve wood but has since been removed from the market due to it being a known carcinogen as well as causing kidney and liver disease, seizures, skin irritation similar to chemical burns, rashes, mental disarray and death. Listed as a known poison and carcinogen by the United States Health and Safety Administration, by the International Agency for Research and the Environmental Protection Agency." The FDA does state that they do not allow "adulterated" meats (such as 4D meat) to be used in animal feed, but a few paragraphs down on the exact same page they mention that they cannot enforce such rules as much as they would like due to a lack of resources. In other words, there's really nothing stopping companies from doing this outside of an unregulated paragraph saying they can't do it.

In that same book, Brady talks about one of the most infamous pet food scandals in modern history: the 2007 melamine scandal. To briefly summarize the scandal, pet food companies were purchasing contaminated wheat gluten and rice protein from China. The manufacturers in China purposefully contaminated the grain with a substance called melamine, which artificially boosts the protein content of animal feed ingredients at a fraction of the price of high-quality protein. Melamine is a chemical derived from coal and is often used in plastic manufacturing, but has become very popular in animal feed in the last few decades. What is even more upsetting about this scandal is the amount of pet food that was affected. Brady writes, "This particular scandal ended up affecting over 100 companies including Menu Foods, Nestle Purina, Hill's Science Diet and Royal Canin (owned by Mars Inc.). In the United States, Australia, Europe and South Africa, 5,300 products and more than sixty million packages of pet food were recalled, highlighting for us the fact that most of these products use the same ingredients and are about as different from each other as fur and hair." To us, this shows that big kibble companies are trying to find ways to cut costs and maximize profits, even at the expense of the health of pets around the world. Not only that, but when contaminations occur at the manufacturing level, and so many companies use the same ingredients and suppliers, switching foods may not even solve the problem.

"In the extrusion process, the dough is heated under pressure, then pushed through a die machine that cuts the kibbles." Many popular brands of kibble are ultra-processed, which means they have gone through several stages of cooking at extremely high pressures. On average, most kibble has been high-heat processed four times and, as many veterinarians and scientists have shown, each time pet food is heated, it "eliminates nutrients and bioactive compounds that prevent disease and degeneration, and it creates biotoxins that accelerate the cellular aging and dying process," according to Dr. Karen Becker and Rodney Habib in their book, *The Forever Dog*. As we talked about earlier, when companies use 4D meat (meat from animals that did not die via slaughter), getting said meat to a point where it's safe to consume requires immense heat and processing.

"Kibble size and shape vary according to the product specification. The kibbles are dried, cooled and spray coated." The last part of that sentence is where we really want to focus; "kibbles are dried, cooled and spray coated." What is the kibble being spray coated with? To make kibble more palatable, manufacturers often add fats and natural or artificial flavors. This is because the high temperatures and multiple cookings used in the kibble production process can negatively affect the flavor and palatability of the feed. To compensate for nutrient losses during the cooking process, manufacturers also add vitamins and minerals to the finished product. In *The Forever Dog*, Becker and Habib go on to talk about advanced glycation end products, or AGEs, writing, "AGEs created through high-heat processing rapidly age our dogs and create disease—and our dogs eat massive amounts of these toxic substances every day in ultra-processed pet foods." As you can probably guess, the more heat and processing time food goes through, the more AGEs are created. The good news is, many companies are becoming aware of this and shifting to a different style of cooking.

"Some dry foods may also be produced by means other than extrusion, such as baking." Now, by this point, you may be freaking out about what you currently feed your dog (we only say this because that's exactly what happened to us), but there is good news! The last part of that sentence, "such as baking", is one method companies are using to dial down the heat and processing time of their pet foods. Other methods include freeze-drying, dehydrating, gently cooking and air-drying. These days, you can find many options within each of those categories, and all of those methods are going to be a less-processed, and therefore healthier and more bioavailable, option for your dogs. At the time of writing this book, we feed a blend of raw and gently cooked pet food.

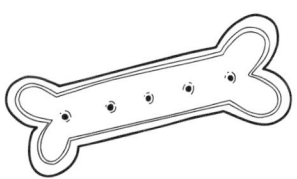

So now, with all of this new information, how is kibble *actually* made? Let's let the wonderful authors of *The Forever Dog* break it down for us: "Animal carcasses are ground up and boiled to separate animal fat from bone and tissue, a process called 'rendering' (first heat adulteration). Bone and tissues are strained and pressed to remove moisture, heat dried (second heat adulteration), and pulverized to make meat meals. Peas, corn, and other veggies you see listed on the label most likely arrived at the pet food plant already dried (via heat) or in powdered form (like pea protein and corn gluten meal). These dry, already-heat-processed ingredients are then blended with other ingredients (that have also been previously cooked and dried) to make a dough that is high-pressure-cooked in an extruder, baked, or air-dried at high temperatures. Extruded kibble is heated a fourth time when it comes out of the extruder to reduce the moisture content, the final step in the process (and at least a fourth heat adulteration). The average bag of dry food contains ingredients that have been high-heat processed at least four times. It is literally dead food."

As we've stated before, none of the information in this book is shared with the intent of shaming or making you feel bad about what you do. Fresh feeding is still an incredibly privileged way for humans to eat, but especially for our animals to be eating. If you can't feed anything other than kibble, we have tons of tips throughout this book to boost your dog's meals without breaking the bank. You're a wonderful pet parent just for being here, and we'll be sure to teach you everything we know.

## BETTER OPTIONS FOR YOUR DOG

Now that we have established how kibble is made, it's important to note that not all kibbles are made equally. There are several companies working to create a better product that is still shelf-stable without cutting corners for the sake of a cheaper ingredient. If we were at the store trying to find the healthiest option available, there are a few things we would look out for:

## Things to Look for in Kibble

- Look for a lot of named meats (e.g., beef heart or pork liver, rather than meat/bone meals) near the top of the ingredient list so you know the bulk of the calories are coming from animal sources of protein and other nutrients.

## Things to Avoid in Kibble

- Avoid ingredient splitting, which is when a company takes an ingredient like peas, for example, and splits it up into pea protein, pea fiber and pea flour, rather than just listing peas. They do this so they can make peas look like they make up a smaller percentage of the overall food than they actually do. If you have 21 pounds (9.5 kg) of peas and 8 pounds (3.6 kg) of chicken, you can split the peas into three categories and then claim chicken is the number one ingredient.

- Avoid potentially carcinogenic, synthetic preservatives like BHA, BHT and ethoxyquin.

- Avoid artificial colors like Red 40, Yellow 5 and 6 and Blue 2.

- Avoid corn. Corn isn't necessarily unhealthy, but it's a common, cheap filler in many of the most popular kibble brands. It's often used because it's a good source of energy (but so are donuts—doesn't mean they're healthy) and cheaper than high-quality meats. Dogs have no biological need for any sort of carbohydrate in their diet.

- Avoid added sugars, such as molasses, brown sugar and granulated sugar. Sugar in small quantities (like treats) isn't a bad thing, but it's not something you want in every meal you feed your dog.

- Avoid excess carbohydrates. Carbs are not necessarily bad for dogs, but high-glycemic, highly processed carbs may be at the root of many common ailments our dogs go through. You want your kibble to have many named meats like beef heart and chicken liver before carbs start showing up. Dogs have evolved over thousands of years to become carnivorous animals, with a digestive system that is well suited to digesting meat and bone. Their sharp teeth, powerful jaws and short intestines are all adaptations that allow them to efficiently process and extract nutrients from animal proteins and fats. Dogs have no biological need for carbohydrates and can thrive on a diet that is rich in animal products alone.

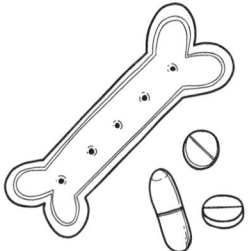

Chapter 2

# HOW TO IMPROVE YOUR DOG'S CURRENT FOOD

When it comes to improving your dog's diet, it doesn't have to be all or nothing. We recognize that feeding a fully fresh diet, whether it be raw, gently cooked or freeze-dried, is an immense privilege that the majority of pet parents don't have access to. Because of this fact, it has become one of our missions to make fresh feeding and improving your dog's diet accessible for everyone, regardless of your budget. Your dog can receive so many benefits by simply boosting their kibble with specific foods and supplements and replacing a small portion of highly processed food with whole, natural ingredients.

# MEAL BOOSTERS AND SUPPLEMENTS
## Hydration

For every pet parent new to improving their dog's kibble, this is the perfect place to start. It's the easiest way to make a big change, and if you use water (we recommend filtered water), it's almost free. Kibble generally has 70 to 80 percent less water than fresh food does. Remember reading about how kibble is heated four separate times? That removes almost all traces of moisture. Kibble-fed dogs have to make up for the lack of hydration in their diet by drinking it from their water bowl, which doesn't sound like a bad thing, but remember they have bodies that evolved over millions of years eating fresh, live foods full of moisture and not relying solely on drinking water to stay hydrated.

There are many things you could hydrate your dog's kibble with, but a few of our favorites are bone broth (page 121) and coconut water. If you are purchasing these products, be sure to avoid added sugars, gums, onions, sodium, artificial flavors/colors and xylitol/birch sugar. The fewer the ingredients (and the more you can pronounce), the better. There are also brands that make dog-specific versions of these items, but they tend to be more expensive. Regardless of what you choose, always check the ingredient list first. Once you have chosen your hydration product, simply pour enough of it into your dog's bowl to cover the kibble, and optionally you can let it soak for 10 to 15 minutes to really saturate the food, or simply feed it immediately as sort of a broth with the food.

NOTE: Whenever we share content about hydrating kibble, we always get comments asking if this takes away the teeth-cleaning capabilities of kibble. While bigger kibble pieces have been shown to remove plaque and tartar from a dog's teeth, kibble is still made up primarily of carbohydrates, and carbohydrates are not great for dental health. For this reason, we generally recommend not relying on your dog's kibble to clean their teeth (unless you are feeding a diet featuring raw meaty bones). Teeth cleaning should come in the form of brushing their teeth or giving specific dental chews (and not the ones you'd expect, but more on those in chapter 6).

## Supplements

Another way to boost your dog's kibble is by adding supplements. There are two ways you can supplement your dog's kibble: using fresh foods or using synthetic sources. For example, a fresh food source of glucosamine is found in green-lipped mussels, but you can also feed a glucosamine supplement in a pill, chew or multivitamin. Of course, fresh sources for everything will always be preferred (at least in our opinion), as whole foods generally have the most biologically available nutrients. However, we recognize that so many people don't have access to some if not many of these fresh food sources, and that's where synthetic supplements can be very beneficial.

When we use supplements, we try to use them intentionally. Here are some of our favorites, why we use them and their fresh and synthetic sources.

| Supplements | | |
|---|---|---|
| **Supplement Type** | **Benefits** | **Fresh Source** |
| Probiotics | Probiotics can be beneficial for dogs in several ways. First and foremost, they help support your dog's immune system, which can help prevent a wide range of illnesses. Probiotics can also support your dog's digestive system, which can help improve your dog's overall health and immune system. Probiotics can also reduce the risk of gastrointestinal problems, such as diarrhea, constipation and gas. Additionally, probiotics can support the growth of good bacteria in your dog's gut, which can help maintain a healthy balance of bacteria in the gut. | • Raw goat milk<br>• Yogurt and other fermented dairy products, such as kefir<br>• Fermented vegetables, like sauerkraut<br>• Kombucha<br>• Some fruit juices and drinks, such as apple cider vinegar and coconut water |
| Omega-3 Fatty Acids | These fatty acids can help improve your dog's coat and skin health, reduce inflammation and support joint health. They can also support the immune system and improve cognitive function. | • Green-lipped mussels<br>• Oily fish, such as sardines, salmon and mackerel |

## Supplements

| Supplement Type | Benefits | Fresh Source |
|---|---|---|
| Prebiotics | Prebiotics are nondigestible compounds that stimulate the growth and activity of beneficial bacteria in the gut. Some of the potential benefits of prebiotics in a dog's diet include improved digestion and absorption of nutrients, enhanced immune function and reduced risk of gastrointestinal disorders. Prebiotics may also help maintain a healthy balance of gut bacteria, which is important for overall health and well-being. In addition, prebiotics can provide dietary fiber, which can help promote regular bowel movements and prevent constipation in dogs. | • Nuts and seeds, such as almonds, flaxseed and chia seeds<br>• Fruits, such as apples, berries and pears<br>• Vegetables, such as broccoli, Brussels sprouts and spinach<br>• Root vegetables, such as sweet potatoes, carrots, chicory root/inulin and parsnips |
| Glucosamine | When given to dogs as a supplement, it may help support joint health and mobility, particularly in older dogs or dogs with joint problems. Some studies have also suggested that glucosamine may be effective in reducing inflammation and pain associated with arthritis and other joint conditions. | • Green-lipped mussels<br>• Poultry feet<br>• Beef trachea<br>• Bone broth or chicken broth<br>• Organ meats, such as liver, kidney and gizzards<br>• Eggshell membranes |
| Antioxidants | Antioxidants can help support healthy brain function and may improve cognitive function in dogs. This can be particularly important for older dogs, who may be more susceptible to age-related cognitive decline.<br><br>They can also help protect cells from damage and reduce inflammation in the body. This helps reduce the risk of chronic diseases such as heart disease, cancer and diabetes. Antioxidants can help support healthy skin and a shiny coat. They may also help reduce shedding and promote overall skin health.<br><br>They also help support the body's natural energy production processes, which can help increase your dog's energy and vitality. | • Berries, such as blueberries, strawberries, raspberries and blackberries<br>• Leafy green vegetables, such as spinach, kale and collard greens<br>• Nuts and seeds, such as walnuts, almonds and sunflower seeds<br>• Fatty fish, such as salmon, sardines and mackerel<br>• Green tea<br>• Fruits and vegetables with deep, vibrant colors, such as red peppers, orange carrots and purple eggplant<br>• Mushrooms, such as Reishi, Lion's Mane, Turkey Tail, Chaga, Maitake and Shiitake |

# FEEDING KIBBLE AND FRESH FOOD
## 90/10

Arguably the most budget-friendly way to improve your dog's diet is with the 90/10 rule. In short, you're going to feed 90 percent kibble and 10 percent fresh food. This method works great for people with a tighter budget or limited access to foods generally used in a homemade diet (such as organ meats and seafood). The reason you're only feeding 10 percent fresh food for this method is because at 10 percent, added foods will not "unbalance" your dog's kibble, meaning you don't have to worry about balancing the 10 percent portion. You can feed them foods like ground turkey or beef, chicken feet, blueberries, carrots and any other dog-safe fresh foods (see page 44).

# 50/50

If you find yourself in between not being able to feed a fully fresh diet but wanting to do more than the 90/10 supplementation of kibble, 50/50 is for you. This is where you are feeding 50 percent kibble and 50 percent fresh food. The 50 percent fresh food will have to be balanced (more on balancing on page 58). This 50 percent fresh can be raw, gently cooked, air-dried or freeze-dried.

One tricky part of feeding a 50/50 blend of kibble and fresh food is figuring out how much of each food to feed your dog. To figure out how much kibble and homemade food you need to feed them, follow these simple steps:

1.  Determine how much kibble you need to feed your dog by following the guidelines on the bag.

2.  Cut that number in half to account for the homemade food.

3.  Determine how much fresh food your dog needs to eat by using the information on page 58.

4.  Cut that value in half to account for the kibble.

5.  Feed a combination of kibble and fresh food as one, two or three meals throughout the day.

### Example

Cooper eats 2 cups (metric equivalent varies) of kibble per day if eating just kibble. He eats 20 ounces (560 g) of fresh food per day (based on the equation on page 58) when eating just fresh food. If we want to feed him a 50/50 blend, we would cut those numbers in half, so he would be getting 1 cup of kibble and 10 ounces (280 g) of fresh food per day. But, we also feed him twice a day, so we now have to cut those values in half again to determine how much he eats per meal (divide by three if feeding three meals). This means we will be feeding ½ cup of kibble along with 5 ounces (140 g) of fresh food per meal. Try not to stress about getting the amounts down to the exact thousandth of a cup or ounce. We want to be as close as possible, but feeding our dogs does not have to be so exact like many professionals make it seem.

## Chapter 3

# THE FUNDAMENTALS OF FRESH FEEDING

Imagine walking into your doctor's office for a yearly check-up and your doctor asks you what your diet is like. You tell them you've been eating a lot of fresh fruits and vegetables, grass-fed beef and other whole foods, and they look at you and start explaining how dangerous that is because it could be deficient in certain nutrients. Instead, they point you to their in-hospital store, where they have premade cereals and shakes that claim to be fully balanced with all the nutrients you need, and tell you that you can simply eat that every single day for the rest of your life. It's got some ingredients you recognize, along with dozens that you can't even pronounce. To us, that sounds like a dystopian future that we don't want to live in, but as you are reading this, 94 percent of North Americans feed their dogs kibble, and many of them most likely got the recommendation from their veterinarian.

Now let's pause. You're probably feeling one of two emotions right now: First, you may feel defensive, especially if you work or know someone who works in the veterinary industry, or you may be feeling angry and wondering how someone who takes an oath to heal animals could possibly recommend something like kibble. Bottom line, a lot of this comes down to personal opinion, but our opinion has been shaped by industry leaders, veterinarians and indisputable evidence showing the benefits of a fresh, whole food diet.

Many conventional veterinarians and big kibble manufacturers tout their products as superior because they are "complete and balanced" according to either National Research Council (NRC) guidelines or Association for American Feed Control Officials (AAFCO) recommendations. There is probably a logical reason for this: Conventional veterinarians likely see many dogs each year that are being fed a nutritionally deficient diet. This can lead to serious health issues, and they probably believe that, while kibble may not be the best diet option, it at least provides the necessary nutrients that dogs need on a daily basis. This is one of the main reasons we are writing this book: to provide pet owners like you with a reliable resource to help you *properly* feed a homemade diet. We hope that this book will make your life, your dog's life and your vet's life easier.

Conventional veterinarians and nutrition experts say that looking at the ingredients in a bag of dog food or treats is not a good way to determine food quality. It seems they are mostly focused on whether or not nutrient levels are met. To us, this is a little bit backwards. Remember reading about the melamine scandal and how manufacturers were artificially boosting the protein levels of foods they were processing? This seems like one gigantic risk of focusing on the nutrient levels rather than the ingredients themselves. We would much rather feed a species-appropriate, whole-food diet that's full of diverse, fresh ingredients and rely on variety feeding to meet our dog's nutritional needs, just like we as humans currently do. Humans don't generally calculate how much calcium and iodine and other vitamins and minerals are in their food to ensure they get the proper amount. We also don't rely on an "all-in-one" formula (which for humans would be similar to baby formula or Soylent) to provide our nutrients. As the experts in human nutrition say, eat the rainbow and shop the outskirts of the stores, not the aisles (because the aisles are where the highly processed food is, including kibble).

Please understand that veterinarians are not recommending kibble because they are out to hurt animals. They are simply recommending what they've been taught in veterinary school. Why are they being taught that kibble is generally a better option in veterinary school? The following example may shed some light on that question.

In one of my (Bryce's) nutrition courses, we used a textbook that is commonly used in veterinary schools across the United States: *Small Animal Clinical Nutrition* by Hand, Thatcher, Remillard, Roudebush and Novotny. It's a giant textbook filled with pretty much everything you could imagine about nutrition and health for small animals. Twenty percent of the editors (one out of five) have ties with Hill's Pet Nutrition (makers of Hill's Science Diet), and 31 of the 115 contributors are associated with at least one big kibble company. Within the textbook, all of the cases we have come across involve situations dealing only with kibble-fed dogs, never dogs on a homemade diet. There are also many aspects that seem to demonize or use fear tactics to push people away from fresh feeding and toward kibble feeding. As we mentioned earlier, there are no limits to the reach that big kibble possesses, and we believe they are highly influential in what veterinarians are learning in veterinary school, FDA regulations and anti-fresh-feeding marketing. Kibble companies also donate large amounts of money to veterinary schools to get teaching time in front of young, impressionable vets. What's needed, in our opinion, is a complete overhaul of veterinary education with a greater emphasis on unbiased, science-based research from sources *outside* of the pet industry.

With all of that being said, there are so many veterinarians who *are* learning the truth about the pet industry and are working tirelessly to increase the number of animals being fed fresh food.

# WHY FRESH FOOD?

If you watch any of our content, you can probably see that we recommend various brands and products within each sector of the pet category. Whether it's treats, chews or raw dog food, we always want to showcase where to get products in different locations, within varied budgets or with different needs altogether. Beyond any brand recommendation, the ultimate goal is to convince more people to feed fresh food. Why? Because countless studies show that the consumption of fresh, whole, nutrient-rich foods is essential for vitality and longevity.

In 2019, the medical journal *The Lancet* found in one of their studies that one out of every five human deaths globally can be attributed to unhealthy diet alone. "Unhealthy" meaning high in sugar, highly processed, full of synthetic ingredients, the list goes on. Because we share about 84 percent of our DNA with dogs (and we both fall under the mammal class), we feel that this directly applies to our canine family members and should be heavily considered when determining what to feed your dog.

# MODELS OF FRESH FEEDING

To us, fresh feeding involves feeding a minimally processed diet of muscle meat, organ meat, bone and other ingredients to help fill nutritional gaps. A few of the most popular raw feeding methods include BARF (Biologically Appropriate Raw Food), The Ancestral Diet, Prey Model Raw and Whole Prey. In reality, there are probably an infinite number of ways you can feed your dog that don't rely on kibble. Rather than trying to identify each and every feeding method, we're going to give you our favorites and the ones most commonly recommended by integrative nutrition professionals.

## BARF or Biologically Appropriate Raw Food

This is a diet made up of 70 percent muscle meat, 5 percent liver, 5 percent other secreting organs, 10 percent bone, 7 percent vegetables and 3 percent fruits (sometimes 1 percent fruit and 2 percent nuts). Our meal recipes later on in the book are based on the BARF diet, but don't include the nuts and do include a few items that don't fit into the categories listed above.

This diet closely resembles what a wild dog would eat, as they have been observed eating the stomach contents of their prey as well as small amounts of plant matter when prey is limited.

**Example recipe for a 40-pound (18-kg) adult dog's daily food intake (more recipes on page 72):**

- 11 oz (308 g) ground beef
- 1.6 oz (45 g) beef short ribs
- 0.8 oz (22 g) beef liver
- 0.8 oz (22 g) beef kidney
- 1.1 oz (31 g) steamed broccoli
- 0.45 oz (13 g) blueberries

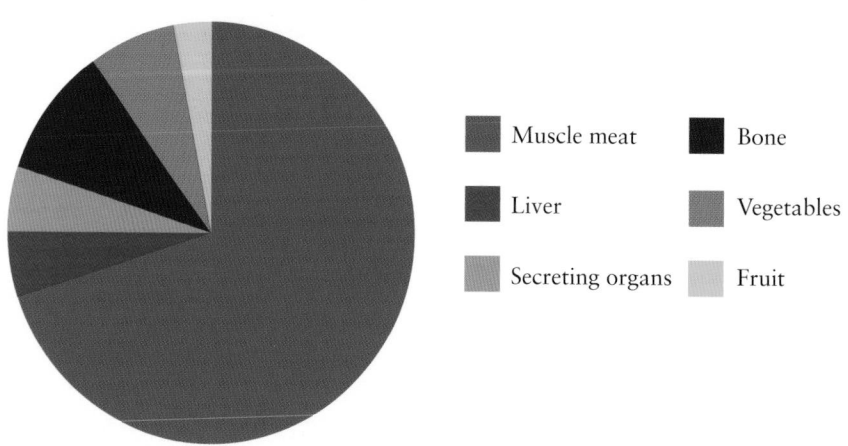

Muscle meat | Bone
Liver | Vegetables
Secreting organs | Fruit

## The Ancestral Diet

The Ancestral Diet is commonly made up of 63 percent muscle meat, 10 percent seafood, 12 percent bone, 5 percent liver, 5 percent other secreting organs and 5 percent fiber or fur. It uses a similar base of meaty bone, muscle meat and organ meat, but ancestral feeders generally use fur and some veggies as their fiber source and include a dedicated amount of seafood.

**Example recipe for a 40-pound (18-kg) adult dog's daily food intake:**

- 8.8 oz (246 g) ground beef
- 3.2 oz (90 g) chicken feet
- 1.6 oz (45 g) sardines
- 0.8 oz (22 g) beef kidney
- 0.8 oz (22 g) beef liver
- 0.8 oz (22 g) fur

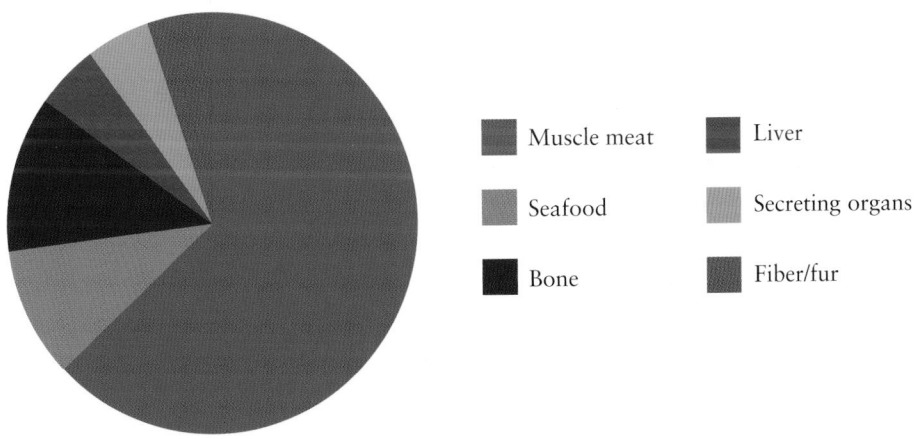

Muscle meat   Liver

Seafood   Secreting organs

Bone   Fiber/fur

## Prey Model Raw

The Prey Model Raw diet is one on which many other diets are based. Essentially, it's 80 percent muscle meat, 5 percent liver, 5 percent other secreting organs and 10 percent bone content. The big criticism of this diet is that it doesn't include all of the nutrients dogs need to thrive. It loosely resembles the makeup of an entire prey animal, but would be missing nutrients dogs get when they eat the skin, stomach lining/contents, various organs and other parts of a whole prey animal. Diets like BARF or Ancestral will take away some of the 80 percent muscle meat in Prey Model Raw and replace it with other foods that help fill nutritional gaps in the meals over time.

**Example recipe for a 40-pound (18-kg) adult dog's daily food intake:**

- 9.6 oz (269 g) ground beef
- 4.8 oz (134 g) chicken backs or turkey necks
- 0.8 oz (22 g) beef liver
- 0.8 oz (22 g) beef spleen

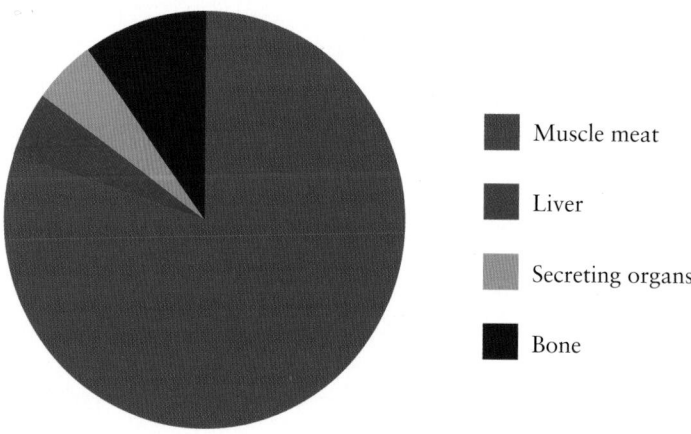

Muscle meat

Liver

Secreting organs

Bone

## Whole Prey

The Whole Prey diet comes the closest to mimicking what our dogs would eat in the wild. It involves exactly what it says: feeding an entire animal as their meal. With this diet, you don't really have to focus on ratios because most raw diets are trying to emulate whole prey. Instead, you just have to focus on the amount you feed and feeding a variety of whole prey animals. These animals tend to be mice, rats, rabbits and small birds like pheasants and chicks.

This is one of the harder feeding methods simply due to sourcing. Finding fresh animals still fully intact is rather difficult, especially if you live in smaller towns with limited access.

# FOODS TOXIC TO DOGS

## Xylitol/Birch Sugar

Xylitol or birch sugar is a sugar substitute that is commonly found in sugar-free gum and other sugar-free products, peanut butter (though most popular brands have stopped using this) and toothpaste. It can cause a rapid insulin release in dogs, leading to low blood sugar and potentially life-threatening liver failure. Symptoms of xylitol poisoning in dogs may include vomiting, loss of coordination and loss of consciousness.

## Chocolate

Chocolate is toxic to dogs because it contains a chemical called theobromine, which is similar to caffeine. Theobromine is a stimulant that can cause rapid heart rate, tremors and seizures in dogs. Dark chocolate and unsweetened baking chocolate contain higher levels of theobromine than milk chocolate and are more likely to be toxic.

## Alcohol

Even small amounts of alcohol can cause problems for dogs, including vomiting, difficulty breathing and even death. In addition, alcohol can interact with certain medications, making them more dangerous for dogs.

## Raw Dough

Raw dough contains yeast, which can cause the dough to rise in the dog's stomach. This can cause uncomfortable bloating and gas, and in severe cases it can lead to a potentially life-threatening condition known as gastric dilation volvulus (GDV), also known as twisted stomach. Yeast also ferments in the digestive tract, creating alcohol, which can lead to alcohol poisoning.

## Onions and Chives

Onions and chives are toxic to dogs because they contain compounds that can damage the dog's red blood cells. When these red blood cells are damaged, they become more fragile and prone to rupture. When enough red blood cells rupture, the dog can develop anemia, which can be dangerous or even fatal if left untreated.

## Grapes and Raisins

Grapes and raisins can be toxic to dogs, although the exact reason why is not well understood. It is thought that a toxic substance is present in grapes and raisins that can damage the kidneys of dogs, leading to potentially serious health problems. This can happen even if the dog only eats a small amount of grapes or raisins. Symptoms of grape or raisin toxicity in dogs can include vomiting, diarrhea, lethargy and loss of appetite. In severe cases, it can lead to kidney failure, which can be fatal if not treated promptly.

## Macadamia Nuts

Macadamia nuts are toxic to dogs because they contain a toxin that can affect the dog's nervous system. This toxin can cause symptoms such as vomiting, tremors and difficulty walking. In severe cases, ingestion of macadamia nuts can lead to hyperthermia, increased heart rate and difficulty breathing.

# DOG-SAFE FOODS

While all of the following foods are safe for dogs, the amount to feed will always vary depending on your dog and their current diet. Work with a holistic veterinarian or certified canine nutritionist to help determine which foods and how much of them will work best for your specific situation.

| Dog-Safe Foods | | | | | |
|---|---|---|---|---|---|
| **Meats** | **Seafood** | **Fruits** | **Vegetables** | **Herbs/Spices** | **Miscellaneous** |
| • Beef<br>• Bison<br>• Chicken<br>• Deer<br>• Duck<br>• Elk<br>• Goat<br>• Kangaroo<br>• Mice<br>• Moose<br>• Ostrich<br>• Rabbit<br>• Sheep/Lamb<br>• Turkey | • Cod<br>• Herring<br>• Mackerel<br>• Mussels<br>• Oysters<br>• Salmon<br>• Sardines<br>• Tuna | • Apples<br>• Apricots<br>• Avocado<br>• Bananas<br>• Blackberries<br>• Blueberries<br>• Cantaloupe<br>• Coconut<br>• Cranberries<br>• Cucumbers<br>• Dragon fruit<br>• Mango<br>• Papaya<br>• Peaches<br>• Pears<br>• Pineapple<br>• Pumpkin<br>• Raspberries<br>• Strawberries<br>• Tomatoes<br>• Watermelon | • Asparagus<br>• Beets<br>• Bell Peppers<br>• Broccoli<br>• Brussels sprouts<br>• Cabbage<br>• Carrots<br>• Cauliflower<br>• Celery<br>• Cremini mushrooms<br>• Garlic*<br>• Green beans<br>• Kale<br>• Lettuce<br>• Peas<br>• Potatoes<br>• Radish<br>• Rutabaga<br>• Spinach<br>• Squash<br>• Sweet potato<br>• Swiss chard<br>• Turnip<br>• Zucchini | • Aniseed<br>• Chamomile<br>• Cilantro<br>• Coriander<br>• Cinnamon<br>• Dill<br>• Fennel<br>• Fenugreek<br>• Ginger<br>• Mint<br>• Neem<br>• Parsley<br>• Rosemary<br>• Sage<br>• Sweet basil<br>• Thyme (no Spanish thyme)<br>• Turmeric | • Chicken, duck and quail eggs<br>• Goat & cow kefir<br>• Goat's milk<br>• Oats |

NOTE: While we love to feed meat raw, we highly encourage you to blend or cook your vegetables. Many fruits can be fed raw, though they are probably better utilized blended, but veggies for sure need to be blended or cooked to aid digestion and nutrient absorption.

## A NOTE ON GARLIC

23 years ago, a study was conducted involving eight mixed-breed dogs. Each dog received a daily dose of 5 grams of garlic per kilogram of body weight for a period of seven days, while the control group was given water instead. To put this into perspective, a 50-pound dog participating in this study would consume approximately 35-40 cloves of garlic per day. In this study, despite the substantial intake of garlic, no dog developed hemolytic anemia. However, the study concluded that garlic could potentially cause hemolytic anemia due to slight blood level changes observed in the dogs after consuming 20-40 times the recommended amount of garlic.

The belief that garlic is toxic to dogs is rooted in the fact that garlic, onions, and other members of the allium family contain a compound called thiosulfate ($Na_2S_2O_3$). Ingestion of large amounts of thiosulfate can lead to oxidative damage to red blood cells and potentially cause hemolytic anemia. While onions contain high levels of thiosulfate, garlic contains only trace amounts.

Four years after the original study, the same researchers published another study concluding that garlic could potentially enhance immune system function and prevent cardiovascular disease in both dogs and humans. A subsequent study in 2018 by the same team also found that aged garlic extract, a more potent form of garlic, did not produce any adverse effects in dogs when administered at the appropriate dosage.

Despite these findings, organizations such as the ASPCA, VCA Hospitals, the AKC, large pet food companies, and pet insurance providers continue to list garlic as highly toxic to dogs and cats and assert that it causes hemolytic anemia. Interestingly, VCA Veterinary Clinics, which is owned by Mars, identifies garlic as a toxic food for dogs, while Mars simultaneously includes garlic in several of its dog food recipes. This contradiction highlights the inconsistent stance on garlic's toxicity within the pet industry.

Although the original study conducted 23 years ago suggested that garlic could potentially cause hemolytic anemia in dogs, subsequent research has demonstrated the potential health benefits of garlic for dogs when consumed in appropriate amounts. Our suggested dosage is ¼ clove per 10 lbs (4.5 kg) of body weight.

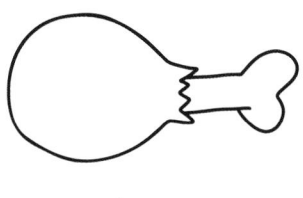

## Chapter 4

# HOW TO FEED YOUR DOG FRESH FOOD FOR OPTIMAL HEALTH

## COMPONENTS OF A HOMEMADE DIET

### Raw Meaty Bones

Raw meaty bones are one aspect of a homemade diet. Because dogs are naturally scavenging carnivores, bone content makes up a small yet essential portion of their diet. Not enough bone could result in runny, loose poops, whereas too much bone can result in hard, chalky poops that are difficult to pass. In most homemade diets, raw meaty bone makes up 8 to 12 percent of the overall diet. We recommend meeting in the middle and doing 10 percent bone content.

NOTE: Feeding raw bones does come with risks, such as choking, splintering and tooth fracture. However, we want you to remember that a dog's body is designed to eat such foods, and there are risks with any treat, chew or food, so always supervise and start slow to ensure they are chewing and eating the bones appropriately.

Raw meaty bones are essential to a dog's diet not just because they need the calcium and phosphorus, but also because they act as a natural toothbrush. Here are many of the benefits of feeding raw meaty bones to your dogs:

- The ripping, tearing and shredding actions scrape plaque and tartar off of teeth to help prevent future dental disease.
- The fibrous tendons within the meat act as a sort of floss to get in between each tooth.
- When your dog crunches on animal parts, it strengthens their jaw muscles and cleans their gums.
- Chewing on meat and bone stimulates your dog's brain and helps expend extra energy, which results in a tired, happy pup.
- Bones help with your dog's own bone growth, supports their joints and can even clear out parasites from the intestinal tract.
- If you have a teething puppy, providing raw meaty bones can drastically improve the pain and discomfort they feel when teeth start ripping through their gums. It also teaches them how to chew on large pieces of food without choking, helps dislodge baby teeth once they're ready to fall out and heals gums where teeth have already fallen out.
- Because raw meaty bones scrape plaque and tartar, bad breath improves because it's removing one of the sources of the foul smell.

In domesticated dogs, it's estimated that 80 percent over the age of three have some form of dental disease. This number is drastically lower when observing wild carnivores like wolves and dingoes, and many attribute this to the fact that wild animals don't have access to starchy carbs that are commonly used in kibble, as well as the dental benefits that come from chewing on raw meat and bone.

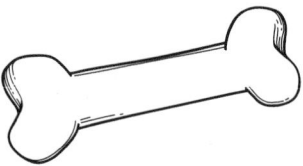

Before you start feeding your dog raw meaty bones, there are a few things you should note. First, your dog's gums may bleed, especially in the beginning. This isn't anything to be overly concerned about, as this is similar to when us humans don't floss for a while and then our gums bleed when we finally do. Repeated feeding of bones (just like repeated flossing) will strengthen the gums and the bleeding should subside. If you are worried about continued bleeding, be sure to consult your veterinarian. The last thing to note is that we *do not* want to be feeding our dogs any cooked bones that are cooked at a high heat, or any weight-bearing bones of large animals (like cows, buffalo and other ungulates) whether they are raw or cooked. Cooked bones have a much greater chance of splintering, and weight-bearing bones are far too hard for dogs to chew, which can result in tooth fractures. Stick to smaller, non-weight-bearing bones (unless they're sourced from animals like poultry or rabbit, which, in that case, is totally fine to feed legs and feet) and only feed raw bones or ones that are gently air-dried at low temperatures (like the ones on page 107), never cooked, smoked or roasted.

## Muscle Meat

In a homemade diet, muscle meat should make up the bulk of the meals. Although the debate is still sticky on whether or not dogs are omnivores, most can agree on the fact that meat should be their main food source. In this book, we recommend feeding about 70 percent muscle meat, and that can and should come from a variety of sources:

- Beef short ribs, heart, tongue, green tripe (never white), lung, ground beef, top loin, top round, bottom round, stew meat
- Lamb heart, ground lamb, loin, lung, shoulder
- Pork shoulder, loin, roast, heart, lung
- Turkey breast, legs, wings, necks, feet, gizzards, ground turkey
- Duck breast, legs, wings, necks, feet, gizzards, ground duck
- Chicken breast, legs, wings, necks, feet, gizzards, ground chicken
- Rabbit are often fed as whole prey when utilized for muscle meat
- Venison shoulder, short ribs, ground venison, heart, lung
- Fish such as anchovies, herring, salmon, sardines, Atlantic mackerel, trout

When you're shopping for cuts of meat for your dog, remember that they don't have as many preferences on texture as we do. Some dogs may not like raw meat on its own, but if they do, opt for the offcuts in stores. Offcuts are the cuts of meat that are not normally used in human meals, as they're tougher and taste different due to the fact that, in many cases, they're more nutrient-dense. Muscle meat offcuts could include heart, cheeks, gizzards, tongue, necks, green tripe (stomach lining), lung, diaphragm and penis. You'll notice that we did list a few organs in the muscle meat section. This is because organs that are non-secreting can be fed the same as regular muscle meat, whereas muscle meats that do secrete are fed in much smaller quantities because of how nutrient-dense they are. If your dog is being picky about raw food, we have found that gently cooked (or even frozen raw) foods can be a big hit instead.

When switching to a homemade diet, one mistake you don't want to make is feeding only muscle meat. In the pet community, many pet parents think that feeding something like chicken, rice and vegetables will be enough, but you will inevitably run into deficiencies down the road. As we stated earlier, muscle meat should make up the bulk of your dog's diet, but muscle meat itself is not balanced, no matter the level of variety you provide. You MUST include organs, bones and other non-meat items (for more on balancing, see page 58).

## Organ Meat

As we mentioned earlier, there are two types of organ meats: secreting and non-secreting. For the organ section of the diet, we always recommend feeding equal parts liver and one other secreting organ (5 percent liver, 5 percent other secreting organ). Hearts, gizzards and other muscle meat organs don't secrete anything and therefore cannot be fed in place of liver/secreting organs. They instead should be fed *alongside* organs as muscle meats.

**Secreting Organs**

- Kidney
- Spleen
- Pancreas
- Testicles
- Uterus
- Thymus
- Eyeballs
- Brain

## Liver

At least 5 percent of the diet must be liver. Liver itself is one of the most nutrient-dense foods on the planet, providing many essential amino acids, vitamins and minerals your dog needs to thrive. Generally, it's recommended to feed liver raw, as it is very heat-sensitive and will lose some nutritional value when it's heated. Livers from different animals have a different nutritional makeup, which is why we stress variety feeding as much as possible.

Organ meat can be one of those foods that is really hard to source. Some of the best places to find it include your local farmers' market, Asian markets and grocery stores, friends who hunt, local butchers and local ranchers. We even found posting on our local Facebook group connected us with many different ethical farmers in our area. They are also the most likely to cut you a deal because you're looking to buy many parts that are often thrown away. There are many companies also selling organ meat and other hard-to-find items online that will ship to you, like Raw Feeding Miami, Texas Tripe and Hare Today.

If you are still having trouble sourcing organ meat, there are many dog treat companies that sell air-dried organ meat, which can easily fit into your homemade diet. You do have to account for weight change once the water is removed, but it's super simple. Air-drying removes about 80 percent of the moisture, so you're going to feed 80 percent less dry organ meat by weight than you would fresh. For example, in our homemade recipes, for a 50-pound (22.7-kg) dog, we recommend feeding 1 ounce (28 g) of fresh liver or 0.2 ounce (6 g) of dried liver. Simply take how much you should feed fresh and multiply it by 0.2 to get the amount you need to feed dry.

## Nonmeat Foods

A diet consisting solely of muscle meat, organ meat and bone is still not nutritionally balanced and will inevitably lead to deficiencies in your dog. To make sure they're getting everything they need, we rely on a few key ingredients with nutrients not found in animals (at least not the parts we have access to in grocery stores). The 80/10/10 or Prey Model Raw diets are commonly deficient in the following nutrients:

| Nutrient Deficiencies | |
|---|---|
| **Nutrient** | **Source** |
| Omega-3 fatty acids | Small, oily fish like mackerel, sardines, herring |
| Chloride | Seaweed |
| Copper | Beef liver, oysters, tahini, spinach |
| Zinc | Oysters, mussels, beef, poultry, pork |
| Manganese | Oysters, mussels, spinach, pineapple |
| Iodine | Seaweed, oysters, eggs, beef liver, chicken, yogurt, kefir |
| Vitamin D | Small, oily fish like mackerel, sardines, herring; beef liver; egg yolks; salmon |
| Vitamin E | Collard greens, spinach, pumpkin, red bell pepper, asparagus, mango, avocado, wheat germ oil |
| Vitamin K | Green, leafy vegetables like spinach and collard greens; broccoli; kale; Brussels sprouts; cabbage |
| Vitamin B$_1$ | Pork; small, oily fish like mackerel, sardines, herring; green peas; yogurt; kefir |

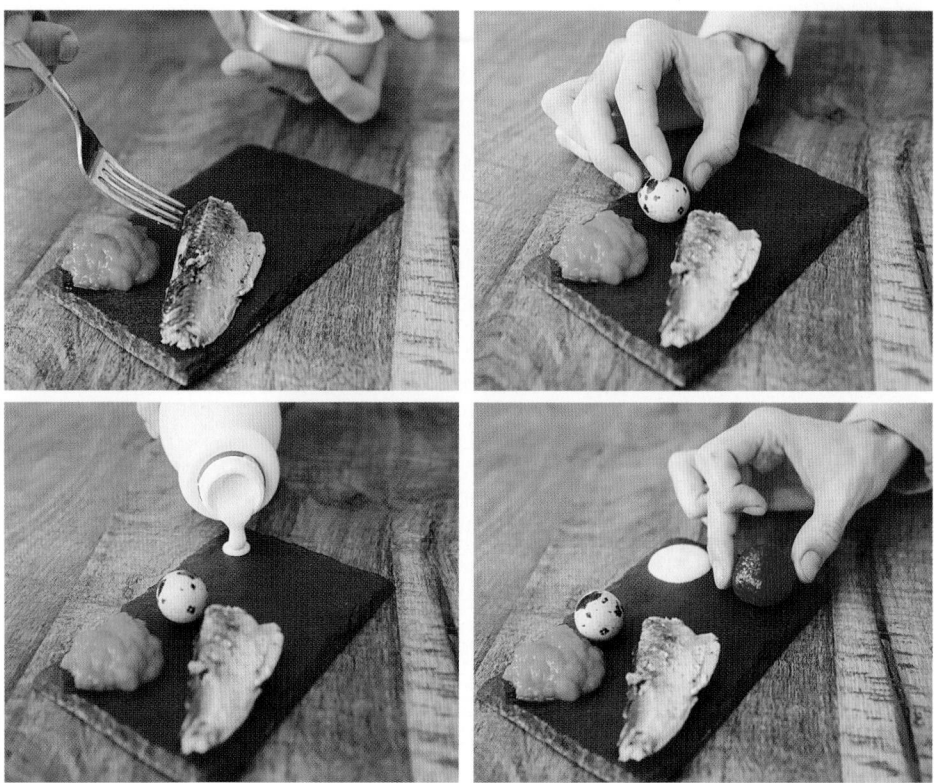

As you can see, there are so many foods that fit into so many categories. It's overwhelming, to say the least! This is why we preach variety feeding so much. Yes, we need to keep the ratios of meat, bone and other foods about the same (see page 58), but within those ratios, we simply focus on feeding the widest variation of ingredients that we can. If you want to feed mussels, feed green-lipped mussels for some meals and blue mussels for others.

When looking at vegetables and other sources of fiber and energy, we can't always just feed it in its raw state. Because dogs have a body designed to consume animal products, they are not very good at utilizing nutrients within plant products. They don't produce the same salivary enzymes that humans do to begin the digestive process of carbs. This means they need a little bit of help, which comes in the form of blending or gently cooking vegetables and other carbs.

# HOW TO BALANCE A HOMEMADE DIET

To balance a homemade diet, we need to use specific ratios for each food group within our BARF variation diet, which includes 70 percent muscle meat, 10 percent bone, 7 percent vegetables, 5 percent liver, 5 percent other secreting organs, 2 percent fruit and 1 percent miscellaneous. By loosely sticking to these ratios and feeding as diverse a diet as possible, you will ensure that all of your dog's nutritional needs are being met.

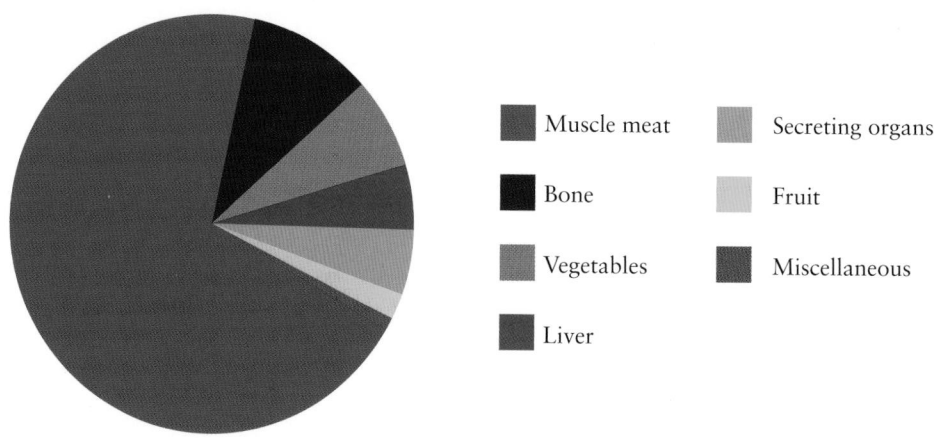

| | | | |
|---|---|---|---|
| ■ Muscle meat | | ▨ Secreting organs | |
| ■ Bone | | ▧ Fruit | |
| ■ Vegetables | | ■ Miscellaneous | |
| ■ Liver | | | |

You'll need to do a quick calculation to figure out how much you're going to feed your dog. For healthy dogs at their ideal weight, you generally feed 2.5 percent of their body weight in ounces (for fresh food only, not dry). To calculate that, take their weight (for example, 50 pounds [22.7 kg]) and multiply that by 0.025 (50 x 0.025, or 2.5 percent) to get your feeding amount in pounds (50 x 0.025 or 2.5 percent = 1.25 pounds [567 g]). You then multiply that by 16 (because 16 ounces = 1 pound [454 g]) to get your feeding amount in ounces (1.25 x 16 = 20 ounces [567 g]). So, for a 50-pound (22.7-kg) dog, you would feed 20 ounces (567 g) of the above food per day.

WEIGHT X 0.025 = FEEDING AMOUNT (LBS)

FEEDING AMOUNT (LBS) X 16 = FEEDING AMOUNT (OUNCES)

If your dog is a different weight, simply plug their weight in pounds into the first part of this paragraph and follow the rest of the steps like normal. If your dog needs to gain weight, or if they are highly active (such as working dogs), you would feed 3 percent of their body weight in ounces, and if they need to lose weight, or if they are not very active at all, you would feed 2 percent of their body weight in ounces. Very small dogs sometimes eat as much as 4 percent of their body weight, whereas very large dogs can eat as little as 1.5 percent of their body weight. It will be a bit of trial and error to see what works best for your individual dog.

Now that we know that our 50-pound (22.7-kg), moderately active dog needs to eat 20 ounces (567 g) of food per day, we need to ensure that that 20 ounces (567 g) has all the nutrients they need. To do that, we want to multiply each food category percentage by 20 ounces (567 g):

- **Muscle meat:** 70 percent (or 0.7) x 20 oz = 14 oz (396 g)
- **Bone:** 10 percent x 20 oz = 2 oz (57 g)
- **Vegetables:** 7 percent x 20 oz = 1.4 oz (40 g)
- **Liver:** 5 percent x 20 oz = 1 oz (28 g)
- **Other secreting organs:** 5 percent x 20 oz = 1 oz (28 g)
- **Fruit:** 2 percent x 20 oz = 0.4 oz (11 g)
- **Miscellaneous:** 1 percent x 20 oz = 0.2 oz (6 g)

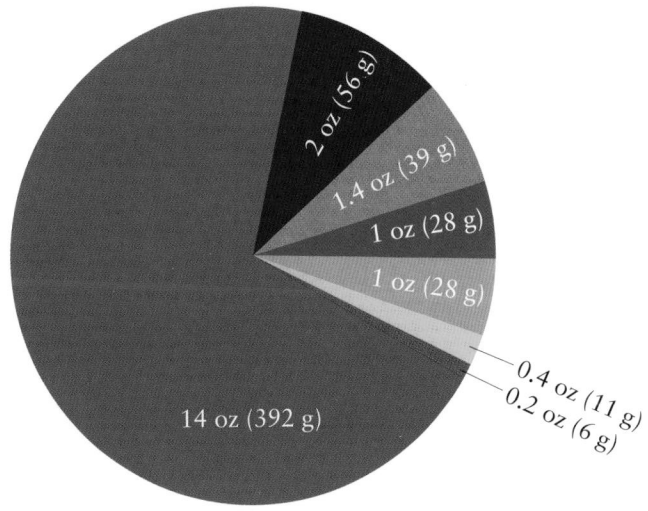

Although we should strive to stick closely to these figures, we vary it a little bit based on what we have in the house, what we have access to and what our dogs' needs are. These guidelines and the recipes later on in the book are not a "one size fits all" equation, but instead are starting points to help you develop a diet specific to your dog. Every single dog is an individual with different needs, and only you and your veterinarian or nutritionist will be able to determine *exactly* what those needs are for your specific dog.

Another aspect of homemade feeding that can be stressful is calculating the meat and bone content of the raw meaty bone you are feeding. When integrating raw meaty bones into your dog's diet, you have to consider the amount of meat that surrounds the bone and factor that into the amount of muscle meat that you are feeding. This can be kind of intimidating, so if you don't want to calculate this yourself, use a raw feeding calculator, like feedreal.com/calculator. This allows you to choose which raw meaty bones you have access to and it will calculate exactly how much of that raw meaty bone and muscle meat you need to feed, without you needing to worry about the bone-to-meat ratio. We also have recipes starting on page 67 that were developed so you don't have to do the calculations yourself.

If you want to, you can search the internet for the ratios of meat to bone for common cuts and do the calculation yourself. Let's say you're using 10 ounces (280 g) of chicken wings. Chicken wings are 54 percent muscle meat and 46 percent bone (according to our internet search), so you'd multiply the total weight by each percentage (10 ounces x 0.54 and 10 ounces x 0.46) and end up with 5.4 ounces (151 g) of muscle meat and 4.6 ounces (129 g) of bone from your 10 ounces (280 g) of chicken wings.

# HOW TO TRANSITION TO A NEW FOOD

When transitioning your dog from one food to another, especially if you're transitioning from kibble to fresh food, you want to take it pretty slow. Ideally, it should be done over a period of seven to ten days to allow their digestive system to adjust. To do this, you gradually increase the amount of new food in their diet by 25 percent every two or three days. For example, on days 1 to 3, you would feed 25 percent new food and 75 percent old food. Days 4 to 6 will be 50/50. Days 7 to 9 will be 75 percent new food and 25 percent old food, and then day 10 will be 100 percent new food. It's important to pay attention to your dog's bowel movements during this process. If they do not have solid poops, do not move on to the next stage of increasing the amount of new food. This process can take longer for some dogs, and it's important to be patient and make adjustments as needed to ensure a smooth transition.

## Chapter 5

# ALTERNATIVE DIETS TO KIBBLE AND RAW FEEDING

## GENTLY COOKED FOOD

Gently cooked food, simply put, means using some amount of heat to process food and rid it of bacteria, but doing so without using *high heat*, such as the processing method that kibble goes through. Generally, gentle cooking involves dehydrating, air-drying, steaming, slow-cooking or some other low-temperature cooking method. It's super convenient and minimizes the risk of foodborne illness for those that are immune compromised or at higher risk of foodborne illness as it pertains to raw meat.

With any sort of heat processing, you're going to have some nutrient loss. At about 158°F (70°C), food starts to lose the enzymes that help a dog digest it, but gently cooking removes far fewer nutrients than high-heat cooking over 500°F (260°C), like kibble.

There is one food you never want to cook above about 160°F (70°C), and that is bone. All bones have the chance to splinter, even if they are raw, but raw and gently air-dried bones (again, under 160°F [70°C]) have a much lower chance of splintering. So, the higher the temperature bones are cooked at, the higher the chance of them splintering because they become brittle as they heat up and dry out. *To ensure there is minimal risk of splintering when feeding them, never roast, boil, smoke or otherwise cook bones above 160°F (70°C).* This is where dehydrators come in handy because ovens sometimes don't go lower than 200°F (93°C). You can find dehydrators online for about $50.

Many companies are starting to sell minimally processed, gently cooked dog food, which can be a great choice for those without the time to make food at home. They are generally more expensive, and often are higher in carbohydrate content than the recipes you'll find in this book, but we feel they are still far better options than highly processed kibble.

# FREEZE-DRIED FOOD

Freeze-dried food is one of the fastest growing types of kibble alternatives. Freeze-drying involves taking already frozen food and placing it inside a vacuum. This allows the water to vaporize, meaning it turns directly from a solid into a gas, skipping the liquid state. The vacuum removes 99 percent of moisture from the food itself, while retaining more nutrients than most other processing methods (because minimal heat is used). For comparison, dehydrating and air-drying removes anywhere from 80 to 90 percent moisture.

Because of the nutrient retention and the fact that the food is now shelf-stable, freeze-dried dog food is a fantastic way for new pet parents to switch from a highly processed kibble to a semi-fresh, minimally processed pet food, while keeping shelf-stability. One drawback is the fact that it takes an enormous amount of energy to run these machines and they are quite expensive to get your hands on personally. We're talking around $4,000 for a used one that fits on your counter. This also factors into the cost of the food, making it one of the more expensive diet choices.

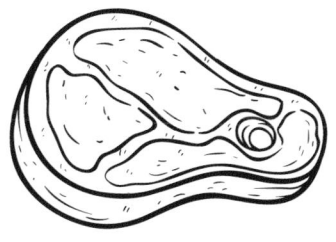

## Chapter 6

# HOMEMADE RECIPES

## INTRODUCTION TO HOMEMADE MEALS

To us, the best diet a healthy, adult dog could eat is a fully raw, diverse, whole-food diet consisting of humanely raised animals and organic, locally grown plant products. Obviously, this is not super attainable or accessible for a large majority of the world, and no one diet suits all dogs (not even raw), so we're going to do the best we can with what we have access to. In this chapter, you'll see many different recipes of raw and gently cooked food. While you don't have to change foods every single day, feeding three to five proteins each week and a healthy variety of plant products and superfoods will ensure nothing is deficient in your dog's diet. We also highly recommend doing biannual or annual blood work with your veterinarian to ensure your dog remains in good health and that you are providing appropriate nutrient levels in their diet.

## FAQ

### Are the meals "complete and balanced"?

"Complete and balanced" generally refers to guidelines set forth by either the National Research Council (NRC) or the American Association for Feed Control Officials (AAFCO). Although these meals have been approved by Dr. Judy Morgan, DVM, CVA, CVCP, CVFT, each meal will not be perfectly balanced to NRC or AAFCO standards. This is because our food philosophy is that we don't feel the need to micromanage our dog's diet down to the gram. Instead, we focus on variety feeding and diversifying each ingredient as much as we can, just like we do for ourselves and our human children. If you feed a variety diet like the raw or gently cooked recipes in this book, your dog should be getting everything they need from their food. If you are worried about deficiencies in your dog's diet, we have a few recommendations. First, you can get regular testing done to check your dog's levels and ensure they don't have any nutrient deficiencies (this is what we do). Your veterinarian can tell you what they are deficient in and should be able to help you supplement their diet accordingly. Another option is to include a multivitamin that is designed to fill nutritional gaps in a homemade diet; check thebkpets.com for our latest multivitamin recommendation. Multivitamins are great for puppies, as growing puppies need all of their required nutrients every day, while adult dogs can receive their required nutrients over the span of a week, max. Lastly, work with your vet. Even if they are against raw or homemade feeding, tell them that you want to do this correctly with their help, and most will be more than happy to assist you.

### Will these recipes automatically work for my dog?

These recipes will most likely work for your dog, but remember that every single dog is an individual and diet and nutrition should be tailored to that individual. Our hope is that this gives you a proper base of knowledge to start cooking meals for your dog at home, and allows you to customize these recipes with the help of your veterinarian or nutritionist to include or exclude certain foods that your dog should or should not have. This will be a trial-and-error process, but with time and patience, you'll find a system that works for you and your pup.

## Is feeding raw food dangerous?

While feeding your dog a raw diet can be a healthy and nutritious option, it's important to be aware of the potential risks and take steps to minimize them. Some of the risks associated with raw feeding include bacterial contamination, exposure to harmful pathogens and choking on raw meaty bones. To prevent choking, it's important to supervise your dog while they are eating bones and intervene if necessary. Additionally, choose bones that are appropriate for your dog's size and chewing abilities. To make raw feeding safer, you can take steps such as sourcing the raw meat from reputable sources and handling it properly to avoid contamination. It's also important to note that those who are immunocompromised or at a higher risk for foodborne illnesses should consider having someone else handle any raw meat as an extra precaution. As we stated earlier, gently cooking is still far healthier than a highly processed kibble, so don't feel bad if you can't or don't want to feed a fully raw diet. Despite the potential risks, many dog owners find that the benefits of raw feeding, such as improved digestion and dental health, outweigh the drawbacks. By taking these precautions, you can help ensure that your dog enjoys the benefits of a raw diet without unnecessary risks.

## How do I handle raw meat safely?

To safely handle raw meat and avoid foodborne illness, it is important to follow a few basic steps. First, be sure to wash your hands thoroughly with soap and warm water before and after handling raw meat. Next, keep raw meat separate from other foods in the refrigerator and use separate cutting boards, utensils and dishes for raw meat to prevent cross-contamination. Lastly, promptly store any leftovers in the refrigerator or freezer to prevent bacterial growth.

### How long does meat last in the refrigerator and freezer?

The shelf life of raw meat depends on the type of meat and how it is stored. In general, raw meat can last anywhere from a few days to a week in the refrigerator, depending on the type of meat and the temperature of the fridge. For example, raw ground meat, poultry and seafood should be used within one or two days, while whole cuts of beef, pork or lamb can last three to five days. Raw meat can also be stored in the freezer for a longer period of time. When properly stored in the freezer, raw meat can last for several months.

### Are the recipes just one meal or one day's worth of food?

The meal recipes in this book are formulated for a 50-pound (22.7-kg) dog's daily intake. This means that if you feed two meals per day and your dog is also 50 pounds (22.7 kg), you would split the recipe in two. If you only feed one meal per day and have a 50-pound (22.7-kg) dog, you feed the entire recipe once. To calculate how much food your dog needs based on their weight, use the equation on page 58 or the tables underneath each meal recipe.

### Can I cook the raw recipes?

You can! We talk about how to cook each food category on page 83, but just make sure you are cooking the food and then measuring it by weight, rather than measuring it by weight raw, and then cooking it. We like to cook any foods we plan on cooking right when we get home from the store, and then store them for meal prepping later.

### Can I make substitutions?

Absolutely! The recipes on the following pages offer a great variety of proteins, fruits, vegetables and superfoods, but if you feel like you want to substitute something in a recipe with another ingredient you have access to, by all means do it! You'll find you have different access to certain foods, and you may need to swap things like chicken eggs for quail eggs if you have a smaller dog, for example. As long as it is dog-safe, we encourage you to always swap out old ingredients for new ones for the sake of variety feeding. Just make sure you are sticking closely to the ratios we have listed here.

| Substitutions | | | | | | |
|---|---|---|---|---|---|---|
| **70 percent** | **10 percent** | **7 percent** | **5 percent** | **5 percent** | **2 percent** | **1 percent** |
| Muscle Meat | Bone | Vegetables | Liver | Other Secreting Organs | Fruit | Miscellaneous |
| • Chicken<br>• Turkey<br>• Beef<br>• Pork<br>• Lamb<br>• Rabbit<br>• Quail<br>• Cornish game hen<br>• Duck<br>• Venison | • Chicken necks<br>• Turkey necks<br>• Rabbit ribs<br>• Quail wings<br>• Duck wings<br>• Cornish game hen carcasses<br>• Pork rib bones<br>• Lamb rib bones<br>• Beef rib bones<br>• Chicken backs | • See page 44 | • No replacing liver | • Spleen<br>• Kidney<br>• Pancreas<br>• Thymus<br>• Ovaries<br>• Testicles<br>• Brain<br>• Eyeballs | • See page 44 | • Kelp<br>• Fish oil<br>• Other foods used to fill nutrient gaps |

As a reminder, if you need to substitute dried products for fresh ones, simply use 20 percent of the dry item in place of the fresh one. During air-drying or dehydrating, meat loses about 80 percent moisture, so 0.2 ounce (6 g) of dried liver will have about the same amount of vitamins and minerals as a 1-ounce (28-g) piece of fresh liver (there is some nutrient loss with any heat processing). All you do is multiply the recommended fresh amount by 0.2 to get your dry total.

## How do I figure out how much to feed my dog?

See page 58 to determine how much to feed your dog, or use the tables underneath each meal recipe.

# RAW MEALS

## BEEF AND CHICKEN

This recipe is one of our favorites for new pet parents just starting out with raw food. Most of the food items can be purchased from local grocery stores, with the exception of organ meat and mussels. These are best found at Asian markets and local butchers.

Ground beef (12.6 oz [353 g])

Chicken feet (3.4 oz [95 g] fresh or 0.68 oz [19 g] dry)

Beef liver (1 oz [28 g] fresh or 0.2 oz [6 g] dry)

Beef kidney (1 oz [28 g] fresh or 0.2 oz [6 g] dry)

Steamed red bell pepper (1.7 oz [48 g])

Blueberries (0.5 oz [14 g])

Sardines (1 oz [28 g] fresh or 0.2 oz [6 g] dry)

Raw goat milk (1 tbsp [15 ml])

Green-lipped mussels (1 oz [28 g] fresh or 0.2 oz [6 g] dry)

Storage: We recommend storing any of your dog's meals in airtight containers in the fridge or freezer. Meals will generally last 2 to 4 days in the fridge and 3 to 4 months in the freezer.

Dosage: If your dog does not weigh one of the weights on the next page, see page 58 to determine your dog's daily food requirement based on their exact weight.

## Proportions by Weight

| | 20 lb (9 kg) | 40 lb (18 kg) | 60 lb (27 kg) | 80 lb (36 kg) | 100 lb (45 kg) | 120 lb (54.5 kg) |
|---|---|---|---|---|---|---|
| Ground Beef | 5.04 oz (141 g) | 10.08 oz (282 g) | 15.12 oz (423 g) | 20.16 oz (565 g) | 25.2 oz (714 g) | 30.24 oz (857 g) |
| Chicken Feet | 1.36 oz (38 g) fresh or 0.27 oz (8 g) dry | 2.72 oz (76 g) fresh or 0.54 oz (15 g) dry | 4.08 oz (114 g) fresh or 0.82 oz (23 g) dry | 5.44 oz (152 g) fresh or 1.09 oz (31 g) dry | 6.8 oz (190 g) fresh or 1.36 oz (38 g) dry | 8.16 oz (229 g) fresh or 1.63 oz (46 g) dry |
| Beef Liver | 0.4 oz (11 g) fresh or 0.08 oz (2 g) dry | 0.8 oz (22 g) fresh or 0.16 oz (4 g) dry | 1.2 oz (34 g) fresh or 0.24 oz (7 g) dry | 1.6 oz (45 g) fresh or 0.32 oz (9 g) dry | 2 oz (56 g) fresh or 0.4 oz (11 g) dry | 2.4 oz (67 g) fresh or 0.48 oz (13 g) dry |
| Beef Kidney | 0.4 oz (11 g) fresh or 0.08 oz (2 g) dry | 0.8 oz (22 g) fresh or 0.16 oz (4 g) dry | 1.2 oz (34 g) fresh or 0.24 oz (7 g) dry | 1.6 oz (45 g) fresh or 0.32 oz (9 g) dry | 2 oz (56 g) fresh or 0.4 oz (11 g) dry | 2.4 oz (67 g) fresh or 0.48 oz (13 g) dry |
| Steamed Bell Pepper | 0.68 oz (19 g) | 1.36 oz (38 g) | 2.04 oz (57 g) | 2.72 oz (76 g) | 3.4 oz (95 g) | 4.08 oz (114 g) |
| Blueberries | 0.2 oz (6 g) | 0.4 oz (11 g) | 0.6 oz (17 g) | 0.8 oz (22 g) | 1 oz (28 g) | 1.2 oz (34 g) |
| Sardines | 0.4 oz (11 g) fresh or 0.08 oz (2 g) dry | 0.8 oz (22 g) fresh or 0.16 oz (4 g) dry | 1.2 oz (34 g) fresh or 0.24 oz (7 g) dry | 1.6 oz (45 g) fresh or 0.32 oz (9 g) dry | 2 oz (56 g) fresh or 0.4 oz (11 g) dry | 2.4 oz (67 g) fresh or 0.48 oz (13 g) dry |
| Goat Milk | ½ tbsp (8 ml) | 1 tbsp (15 ml) | 1 tbsp (15 ml) | 2 tbsp (30 ml) | 2 tbsp (30 ml) | 2 tbsp (30 ml) |
| Mussels | 0.4 oz (11 g) fresh or 0.08 oz (2 g) dry | 0.8 oz (22 g) fresh or 0.16 oz (4 g) dry | 1.2 oz (34 g) fresh or 0.24 oz (7 g) dry | 1.6 oz (45 g) fresh or 0.32 oz (9 g) dry | 2 oz (56 g) fresh or 0.4 oz (11 g) dry | 2.4 oz (67 g) fresh or 0.48 oz (13 g) dry |

# CHICKEN

This is our all-poultry recipe. Much like beef, chicken is a widely available protein at grocery stores and supermarkets, but you may still have some trouble getting the organ meat. As always, hit up your local Asian market, butcher or check out thebkpets.com for our latest organ meat brand suggestions. You'll notice that this recipe is missing that second secreting organ along with the liver. Actually, by feeding heads, you're supplying the other secreting organ with the brain! We've also added some leafy greens, which are great for heart and brain health, as well as cranberries, which are especially good for urinary health and the kidneys.

Chicken breast (13 oz [364 g])

Chicken head (3 oz [84 g] fresh or 0.6 oz [17 g] dry)

Chicken liver (1 oz [28 g] fresh or 0.2 oz [6 g] dry)

Steamed spinach (1.5 oz [42 g])

Seaweed (1 tbsp [5 g] chopped)

Cranberries (0.5 oz [14 g])

Egg (1)

Sardines (1 oz [28 g] fresh or 0.2 oz [6 g] dry)

Oysters (1 oz [28 g] fresh or 0.2 oz [6 g] dry)

Storage: We recommend storing any of your dog's meals in airtight containers in the fridge or freezer. Meals will generally last 2 to 4 days in the fridge and 3 to 4 months in the freezer.

Dosage: If your dog does not weigh one of the weights on the next page, see page 58 to determine your dog's daily food requirement based on their exact weight.

## Proportions by Weight

| | 20 lb (9 kg) | 40 lb (18 kg) | 60 lb (27 kg) | 80 lb (36 kg) | 100 lb (45 kg) | 120 lb (54.5 kg) |
|---|---|---|---|---|---|---|
| Chicken Breast | 5.2 oz (146 g) | 10.4 oz (291 g) | 15.6 oz (437 g) | 20.8 oz (590 g) | 26 oz (737 g) | 31.2 oz (884 g) |
| Chicken Head | 1.2 oz (34 g) fresh or 0.24 oz (7 g) dry | 2.4 oz (67 g) fresh or 0.48 oz (13 g) dry | 3.6 oz (101 g) fresh or 0.72 oz (20 g) dry | 4.8 oz (134 g) fresh or 0.96 oz (27 g) dry | 6 oz (168 g) fresh or 1.2 oz (34 g) dry | 7.2 oz (202 g) fresh or 1.44 oz (40 g) dry |
| Chicken Liver | 0.4 oz (11 g) fresh or 0.08 oz (2 g) dry | 0.8 oz (22 g) fresh or 0.16 oz (4 g) dry | 1.2 oz (34 g) fresh or 0.24 oz (7 g) dry | 1.6 oz (45 g) fresh or 0.32 oz (9 g) dry | 2 oz (56 g) fresh or 0.4 oz (11 g) dry | 2.4 oz (68 g) fresh or 0.58 oz (16 g) dry |
| Steamed Spinach | 0.6 oz (17 g) | 1.2 oz (34 g) | 1.8 oz (50 g) | 2.4 oz (67 g) | 3 oz (84 g) | 3.6 oz (101 g) |
| Seaweed | ½ tbsp (2 g) | 1 tbsp (5 g) | 1 tbsp (5 g) | 2 tbsp (9 g) | 2 tbsp (9 g) | 2 tbsp (9 g) |
| Cranberries | 0.2 oz (6 g) | 0.4 oz (11 g) | 0.6 oz (17 g) | 0.8 oz (22 g) | 1 oz (28 g) | 1.2 oz (34 g) |
| Eggs | ½ | 1 | 1 | 2 | 2 | 2 |
| Sardines | 0.4 oz (11 g) fresh or 0.08 oz (2 g) dry | 0.8 oz (22 g) fresh or 0.16 oz (4 g) dry | 1.2 oz (34 g) fresh or 0.24 oz (7 g) dry | 1.6 oz (45 g) fresh or 0.32 oz (9 g) dry | 2 oz (56 g) fresh or 0.4 oz (11 g) dry | 2.4 oz (68 g) fresh or 0.58 oz (16 g) dry |
| Oysters | 0.4 oz (11 g) fresh or 0.08 oz (2 g) dry | 0.8 oz (22 g) fresh or 0.16 oz (4 g) dry | 1.2 oz (34 g) fresh or 0.24 oz (7 g) dry | 1.6 oz (45 g) fresh or 0.32 oz (9 g) dry | 2 oz (56 g) fresh or 0.4 oz (11 g) dry | 2.4 oz (68 g) fresh or 0.58 oz (16 g) dry |

# TURKEY AND BEEF

**Although these ingredients may be a bit harder to source, dogs without certain protein allergies do really well with mixed and matched animal-based foods. This recipe also features an organ other than liver and kidney, so if you can't find spleen, feel free to use any other secreting organ listed on page 71.**

Ground turkey (11 oz [308 g])

Turkey necks (5 oz [142 g] fresh or 1 oz [28 g] dry)

Beef liver (1 oz [28 g] fresh or 0.2 oz [6 g] dry)

Beef spleen (1 oz [28 g] fresh or 0.2 oz [6 g] dry)

Pumpkin (1.7 oz [48 g])

Pineapple (0.5 oz [14 g])

Blue mussels (1 oz [28 g] fresh or 0.2 oz [6 g] dry)

Ginger (1 tsp [2 g])

Wheat germ oil (2 tsp [10 ml])

Storage: We recommend storing any of your dog's meals in airtight containers in the fridge or freezer. Meals will generally last 2 to 4 days in the fridge and 3 to 4 months in the freezer.

Dosage: If your dog does not weigh one of the weights on the next page, see page 58 to determine your dog's daily food requirement based on their exact weight.

## Proportions by Weight

|  | 20 lb (9 kg) | 40 lb (18 kg) | 60 lb (27 kg) | 80 lb (36 kg) | 100 lb (45 kg) | 120 lb (54.5 kg) |
|---|---|---|---|---|---|---|
| **Ground Turkey** | 4.4 oz (123. g) fresh or 0.88 oz (25 g) dry | 8.8 oz (246 g) fresh or 1.76 oz (49 g) dry | 13.2 oz (370 g) fresh or 2.64 oz (74 g) dry | 17.6 oz (493 g) fresh or 3.52 oz (99 g) dry | 22 oz (624 g) fresh or 4.4 oz (123 g) dry | 26.4 oz (748 g) fresh or 5.28 oz (148 g) dry |
| **Turkey Necks** | 2 oz (56 g) fresh or 0.4 oz (11 g) dry | 4 oz (113 g) fresh or 0.8 oz (22 g) dry | 6 oz (168 g) fresh or 1.2 oz (34 g) dry | 8 oz (224 g) fresh or 1.6 oz (45 g) dry | 10 oz (280 g) fresh or 2 oz (56 g) dry | 12 oz (336 g) fresh or 2.4 oz (67 g) dry |
| **Beef Liver** | 0.4 oz (11 g) fresh or 0.08 oz (2 g) dry | 0.8 oz (22 g) fresh or 0.16 oz (4 g) dry | 1.2 oz (34 g) fresh or 0.24 oz (7 g) dry | 1.6 oz (45 g) fresh or 0.32 oz (9 g) dry | 2 oz (56 g) fresh or 0.4 oz (11 g) dry | 2.4 oz (67 g) fresh or 0.48 oz (13 g) dry |

# PORK AND DUCK

In this pork and duck recipe, we're utilizing duck heads as the bone source. Now, be prepared, duck heads can be a bit graphic to new raw feeders. Rest assured, they are a fantastic bone source, super engaging for your dog to eat and are a part of the duck that is commonly thrown out and wasted. We also include tahini, which is a great source of vitamin E, as well as sardines for the omega-3 fatty acids.

Ground pork (13.1 oz [367 g])

Duck head (2.9 oz [81 g] fresh or 0.58 oz [16 g] dry)

Pork liver (1 oz [28 g] fresh or 0.2 oz [6 g] dry)

Pork kidney (1 oz [28 g] fresh or 0.2 oz [6 g] dry)

Cooked asparagus (1.7 oz [48 g])

Pineapple (0.5 oz [14 g])

Tahini (1 tbsp [14 g])

Yogurt (1 tbsp [15 ml])

Sardines (1 oz [28 g] fresh or 0.2 oz [6 g] dry)

Storage: We recommend storing any of your dog's meals in airtight containers in the fridge or freezer. Meals will generally last 2 to 4 days in the fridge and 3 to 4 months in the freezer.

Dosage: If your dog does not weigh one of the weights on the next page, see page 58 to determine your dog's daily food requirement based on their exact weight.

## Proportions by Weight

| | 20 lb (9 kg) | 40 lb (18 kg) | 60 lb (27 kg) | 80 lb (36 kg) | 100 lb (45 kg) | 120 lb (54.5 kg) |
|---|---|---|---|---|---|---|
| Ground Pork | 5.2 oz (146 g) | 10.4 oz (291 g) | 15.6 oz (437 g) | 20.8 oz (590 g) | 26 oz (737 g) | 31.2 oz (884 g) |
| Duck Head | 1.16 oz (33 g) fresh or 0.23 oz (6 g) dry | 2.32 oz (65 g) fresh or 0.46 oz (13 g) dry | 3.48 oz (97 g) fresh or 0.69 oz (19 g) dry | 4.64 oz (130 g) fresh or 0.93 oz (26 g) dry | 5.8 oz (162 g) fresh or 1.16 oz (33 g) dry | 6.96 oz (195 g) fresh or 1.39 oz (39 g) dry |
| Pork Liver | 0.4 oz (11 g) fresh or 0.08 oz (2 g) dry | 0.8 oz (22 g) fresh or 0.16 oz (4 g) dry | 1.2 oz (34 g) fresh or 0.24 oz (7 g) dry | 1.6 oz (45 g) fresh or 0.32 oz (9 g) dry | 2 oz (56 g) fresh or 0.4 oz (11 g) dry | 2.4 oz (67 g) fresh or 0.48 oz (13 g) dry |
| Pork Kidney | 0.4 oz (11 g) fresh or 0.08 oz (2 g) dry | 0.8 oz (22 g) fresh or 0.16 oz (4 g) dry | 1.2 oz (34 g) fresh or 0.24 oz (7 g) dry | 1.6 oz (45 g) fresh or 0.32 oz (9 g) dry | 2 oz (56 g) fresh or 0.4 oz (11 g) dry | 2.4 oz (67 g) fresh or 0.48 oz (13 g) dry |
| Cooked Asparagus | 0.68 oz (19 g) | 1.36 oz (38 g) | 2.04 oz (57 g) | 2.72 oz (76 g) | 3.4 oz (95 g) | 4.08 oz (114 g) |
| Pineapple | 0.2 oz (6 g) | 0.4 oz (11 g) | 0.6 oz (17 g) | 0.8 oz (22 g) | 1 oz (28 g) | 1.2 oz (34 g) |
| Tahini | ½ tbsp (7 g) | 1 tbsp (14 g) | 1 tbsp (14 g) | 2 tbsp (28 g) | 2 tbsp (28 g) | 2 tbsp (28 g) |
| Yogurt | ½ tbsp (8 ml) | 1 tbsp (15 ml) | 1 tbsp (15 ml) | 2 tbsp (30 ml) | 2 tbsp (30 ml) | 2 tbsp (30 ml) |
| Sardines | 0.4 oz (11 g) fresh or 0.08 oz (2 g) dry | 0.8 oz (22 g) fresh or 0.16 oz (4 g) dry | 1.2 oz (34 g) fresh or 0.24 oz (7 g) dry | 1.6 oz (45 g) fresh or 0.32 oz (9 g) dry | 2 oz (56 g) fresh or 0.4 oz (11 g) dry | 2.4 oz (67 g) fresh or 0.48 oz (13 g) dry |

# BEEF AND DUCK

The last of the five raw meals is our beef and duck recipe. The inclusion of beef heart as the muscle meat is great because, even though we only feed 10 percent secreting organs, whole prey is most likely closer to 25 percent total organs (both secreting and non-secreting) with heart, lungs and other non-secreting organs factored in. If you don't have access to beef heart, feel free to substitute other muscle meats you do have access to.

Beef heart (12.6 oz [353 g])

Duck feet (3.4 oz [95 g] fresh or 0.68 oz [19 g] dry)

Beef liver (1 oz [28 g] fresh or 0.2 oz [6 g] dry)

Beef spleen (1 oz [28 g] fresh or 0.2 oz [6 g] dry)

Cooked sweet potato (1 oz [28 g])

Steamed spinach (0.7 oz [20 g])

Apple (0.5 oz [14 g])

Egg (1)

Sardines (1 oz [28 g] fresh or 0.2 oz [6 g] dry)

Storage: We recommend storing any of your dog's meals in airtight containers in the fridge or freezer. Meals will generally last 2 to 4 days in the fridge and 3 to 4 months in the freezer.

Dosage: If your dog does not weigh one of the weights on the next page, see page 58 to determine your dog's daily food requirement based on their exact weight.

## Proportions by Weight

| | 20 lb (9 kg) | 40 lb (18 kg) | 60 lb (27 kg) | 80 lb (36 kg) | 100 lb (45 kg) | 120 lb (54.5 kg) |
|---|---|---|---|---|---|---|
| Beef Heart | 5.04 oz (141 g) | 10.08 oz (282 g) | 15.12 oz (423 g) | 20.16 oz (572 g) | 25.2 oz (714 g) | 30.24 oz (857 g) |
| Duck Feet | 1.36 oz (38 g) fresh or 0.27 oz (8 g) dry | 2.72 oz (76 g) fresh or 0.54 oz (15 g) dry | 4.08 oz (114 g) fresh or 0.82 oz (23 g) dry | 5.44 oz (152 g) fresh or 1.09 oz (31 g) dry | 6.8 oz (190 g) fresh or 1.36 oz (38 g) dry | 8.16 oz (229 g) fresh or 1.63 oz (46 g) dry |
| Beef Liver | 0.4 oz (11 g) fresh or 0.08 oz (2 g) dry | 0.8 oz (22 g) fresh or 0.16 oz (4 g) dry | 1.2 oz (34 g) fresh or 0.24 oz (7 g) dry | 1.6 oz (45 g) fresh or 0.32 oz (9 g) dry | 2 oz (56 g) fresh or 0.4 oz (11 g) dry | 2.4 oz (67 g) fresh or 0.48 oz (13 g) dry |
| Beef Spleen | 0.4 oz (11 g) fresh or 0.08 oz (2 g) dry | 0.8 oz (22 g) fresh or 0.16 oz (4 g) dry | 1.2 oz (34 g) fresh or 0.24 oz (7 g) dry | 1.6 oz (45 g) fresh or 0.32 oz (9 g) dry | 2 oz (56 g) fresh or 0.4 oz (11 g) dry | 2.4 oz (67 g) fresh or 0.48 oz (13 g) dry |
| Cooked Sweet Potatoes | 0.4 oz (11 g) | 0.8 oz (22 g) | 1.2 oz (34 g) | 1.6 oz (45 g) | 2 oz (56 g) | 2.4 oz (67 g) |
| Steamed Spinach | 0.28 oz (8 g) | 0.56 oz (16 g) | 0.84 oz (24 g) | 1.12 oz (31 g) | 1.4 oz (39 g) | 1.68 oz (47 g) |
| Apple | 0.2 oz (6 g) | 0.4 oz (11 g) | 0.6 oz (17 g) | 0.8 oz (22 g) | 1 oz (28 g) | 1.2 oz (34 g) |
| Egg | 1 | 1 | 2 | 2 | 2 | 3 |
| Sardines | 0.4 oz (11 g) fresh or 0.08 oz (2 g) dry | 0.8 oz (22 g) fresh or 0.16 oz (4 g) dry | 1.2 oz (34 g) fresh or 0.24 oz (7 g) dry | 1.6 oz (45 g) fresh or 0.32 oz (9 g) dry | 2 oz (56 g) fresh or 0.4 oz (11 g) dry | 2.4 oz (67 g) fresh or 0.48 oz (13 g) dry |

# GENTLY COOKED MEALS

## How to Cook Raw Food for Your Dogs

When it comes to cooking meals, we've found that the easiest way is to actually cook it ahead of prepping it. Right after you get home from the store, in fact. What we do is go to the Asian market or butcher or wherever we get our meat, then bring it home and, if necessary, break it down further for cooking. Here is how we prep each food type.

### Muscle Meat

Muscle meat generally comes in two forms: ground meat and whole pieces. With the ground meat, we simply throw it in a pan on the stove and brown it over medium-low to medium heat like you normally would for yourself. Now, with dogs, you're not looking for "crispy" bits, you're just looking for cooked. Getting things to a crisp involves higher heat, which we want to avoid. Once your meat is browned, simply put it in an airtight container and throw it in the fridge or freezer. As a general rule, cooked meat in the fridge will stay good for about 2 to 4 days, and it will stay good in the freezer for about 3 to 4 months.

For muscle meat that isn't ground, we chop it into about 1-inch (2.5-cm) cubes and place them on a baking sheet. We then bake them at 350°F (175°C) until they are completely cooked through, about 15 to 20 minutes. Store the chunked meat just like you would the ground meat above.

### Organ Meat

Organ meat is more susceptible to nutrient loss due to heat exposure than muscle meat. For this reason, we recommend cooking organ meat between 150 and 200°F (66 and 93°C). Dehydrators work best, and many can be purchased online for under $50, but if you don't have access to one, just dehydrate the organ meat in the oven as low as it will go.

The best way to prepare the organ meat for dehydrating is to either slice it thinly, almost like you're making jerky, or puree it in a blender or food processor. Pureeing it allows you to pour it onto your baking sheet and spread it to a super thin consistency (we shoot for ¼ inch [6 mm] thick), which will cause it to dry out faster. Once these are completely dried out (about 4 to 8 hours), they are shelf-stable and will last for 3 months or so. Store the prepared organ meat in an airtight container at room temperature, away from moisture and sunlight, for longest lasting results.

## Vegetables

Dogs don't have the same ability as humans to digest and absorb nutrients from raw vegetables, so we always cook them for our dogs. For things like spinach, kale and other leafy greens, tossing them into a pan over medium heat for 5 to 10 minutes will help break them down. For hardier vegetables like sweet potatoes and carrots, we recommend cutting them into 1-inch (2.5-cm) chunks and baking at 350°F (175°C) for about 15 to 25 minutes, or until they're fork tender. Vegetables can also be blended into smoothie treats, instead of being cooked, as a way of breaking them down for better utilization.

## Seafood

Many seafood items you end up feeding may already be cooked, like canned oysters and mussels, sardines, etc. The ones you don't find already cooked can be baked at 350°F (175°C) for about 15 to 20 minutes, or you can steam them on the stovetop for about the same amount of time, depending on the type of fish you use.

## Fruits

You generally don't need to cook fruits for your dogs. They can be blended into smoothie treats or fed raw.

## Bones

The only way we feel comfortable heat-treating bones is by air-drying under 160°F (70°C; see page 107). The higher the temperature you cook them at, the more likely they are to splinter. Bones that you want to feed should never be roasted, smoked, boiled or otherwise high-heat cooked.

# BEEF AND PORK STEW

This beef and pork stew is a great place to start if you want to feed fresh but don't want to or can't feed raw. With this and all cooked recipes, it's important to note that we are not cooking any of the bones at high heat. If you don't want to feed raw meaty bones, you can dehydrate them at no hotter than 160°F (70°C). Any hotter than this and the bones become more prone to splintering, which is dangerous for dogs.

Beef heart (10 oz [280 g])

Chicken feet (3.4 oz [95 g] fresh or 0.68 oz [19 g] dry)

Green tripe (2.6 oz [73 g] fresh or 0.52 oz [15 g] dry)

Beef liver (1 oz [28 g] fresh or 0.2 oz [6 g] dry)

Pork kidney (1 oz [28 g] fresh or 0.2 oz [6 g] dry)

Bone broth (2.5 oz [74 ml]), or more as needed (page 121)

Avocado (1.7 oz [48 g])

Blackberries (0.5 oz [14 g])

Sardines (1 oz [28 g] fresh or 0.2 oz [6 g] dry)

Tahini (2 tbsp [30 g])

Process and cook all meat and seafood ingredients (if not already cooked) separately (see page 83 for how to do this).

In a dog bowl, combine the beef heart, chicken feet, green tripe, beef liver and pork kidney.

Pour in as much bone broth as needed to turn the meal into a stew.

Top with the avocado, blackberries and sardines.

Drizzle the tahini on top and serve.

Storage: We recommend storing any of your dog's meals in airtight containers in the fridge or freezer. Meals will generally last 2 to 4 days in the fridge and 3 to 4 months in the freezer.

Dosage: If your dog does not weigh one of the weights on the next page, see page 58 to determine your dog's daily food requirement based on their exact weight.

## Proportions by Weight

| | 20 lb (9 kg) | 40 lb (18 kg) | 60 lb (27 kg) | 80 lb (36 kg) | 100 lb (45 kg) | 120 lb (54.5 kg) |
|---|---|---|---|---|---|---|
| Beef Heart | 4 oz (112 g) | 8 oz (224 g) | 12 oz (336 g) | 16 oz (454 g) | 20 oz (567 g) | 24 oz (680 g) |
| Chicken Feet | 1.36 oz (38 g) fresh or 0.27 oz (8 g) dry | 2.72 oz (76 g) fresh or 0.54 oz (15 g) dry | 4.08 oz (114 g) fresh or 0.82 oz (23 g) dry | 5.44 oz (152 g) fresh or 1.09 oz (31 g) dry | 6.8 oz (190 g) fresh or 1.36 oz (38 g) dry | 8.16 oz (229 g) fresh or 1.63 oz (46 g) dry |
| Green Tripe | 1.04 oz (29 g) fresh or 0.21 oz (6 g) dry | 2.08 oz (58 g) fresh or 0.42 oz (12 g) dry | 3.12 oz (87 g) fresh or 0.62 oz (17 g) dry | 4.16 oz (117 g) fresh or 0.83 oz (23 g) dry | 5.2 oz (146 g) fresh or 1.04 oz (29 g) dry | 6.24 oz (175 g) fresh or 1.25 oz (35 g) dry |
| Beef Liver | 0.4 oz (11 g) fresh or 0.08 oz (2 g) dry | 0.8 oz (22 g) fresh or 0.16 oz (4 g) dry | 1.2 oz (34 g) fresh or 0.24 oz (7 g) dry | 1.6 oz (45 g) fresh or 0.32 oz (9 g) dry | 2 oz (56 g) fresh or 0.4 oz (11 g) dry | 2.4 oz (67 g) fresh or 0.48 oz (13 g) dry |
| Pork Kidney | 0.4 oz (11 g) fresh or 0.08 oz (2 g) dry | 0.8 oz (22 g) fresh or 0.16 oz (4 g) dry | 1.2 oz (34 g) fresh or 0.24 oz (7 g) dry | 1.6 oz (45 g) fresh or 0.32 oz (9 g) dry | 2 oz (56 g) fresh or 0.4 oz (11 g) dry | 2.4 oz (67 g) fresh or 0.48 oz (13 g) dry |
| Bone Broth | 1 oz (28 g) | 2 oz (56 g) | 3 oz (84 g) | 4 oz (112 g) | 5 oz (140 g) | 6 oz (168 g) |
| Avocado | 0.68 oz (19 g) | 1.36 oz (38 g) | 2.04 oz (57 g) | 2.72 oz (76 g) | 3.4 oz (95 g) | 4.08 oz (114 g) |
| Blackberries | 0.2 oz (6 g) | 0.4 oz (11 g) | 0.6 oz (17 g) | 0.8 oz (22 g) | 1 oz (28 g) | 1.2 oz (34 g) |
| Sardines | 0.4 oz (11 g) fresh or 0.08 oz (2 g) dry | 0.8 oz (22 g) fresh or 0.16 oz (4 g) dry | 1.2 oz (34 g) fresh or 0.24 oz (7 g) dry | 1.6 oz (45 g) fresh or 0.32 oz (9 g) dry | 2 oz (56 g) fresh or 0.4 oz (11 g) dry | 2.4 oz (67 g) fresh or 0.48 oz (13 g) dry |
| Tahini | 1 tbsp (14 g) | 2 tbsp (28 g) | 2 tbsp (28 g) | 4 tbsp (56 g) | 4 tbsp (56 g) | 4 tbsp (56 g) |

# TURKEY AND PORK STEW

This meal is packed with high-quality protein sources like ground turkey and pork liver, as well as beneficial fruits and vegetables like pumpkin and apple. We've also included some raw goat milk kefir for added probiotics, blue mussels for a boost of omega-3 fatty acids and manganese, and broccoli and apples for the antioxidants.

Ground turkey (12 oz [336 g])

Turkey necks (4 oz [112 g] fresh or 0.8 oz [22 g] dry) (not cooked with the rest)

Pork liver (1 oz [28 g] fresh or 0.2 oz [6 g] dry)

Pork kidney (1 oz [28 g] fresh or 0.2 oz [6 g] dry)

Blue mussels (1 oz [28 g] fresh or 0.2 oz [6 g] dry)

Bone broth (2.5 oz [74 ml], or more as needed) (see page 121)

Pumpkin (1.7 oz [48 g])

Apples (seeds removed) (0.5 oz [14 g])

Scrambled egg (1)

Raw goat milk kefir (1 tbsp [14 ml])

Process and cook all meat and seafood and vegetable ingredients (if not already cooked) separately (see page 83 for how to do this).

In a dog bowl, combine the ground turkey, turkey necks, pork liver, pork kidney and blue mussels.

Pour in as much bone broth as you want to turn the meal into a stew.

Top with the pumpkin, apples and scrambled egg.

Drizzle raw goat milk kefir on top and serve.

Storage: We recommend storing any of your dog's meals in airtight containers in the fridge or freezer. Meals will generally last 2 to 4 days in the fridge and 3 to 4 months in the freezer.

Dosage: If your dog does not weigh one of the weights on the next page, see page 58 to determine your dog's daily food requirement based on their exact weight.

## Proportions by Weight

|  | 20 lb (9 kg) | 40 lb (18 kg) | 60 lb (27 kg) | 80 lb (36 kg) | 100 lb (45 kg) | 120 lb (54.5 kg) |
|---|---|---|---|---|---|---|
| Ground Turkey | 4.8 oz (134 g) | 9.6 oz (269 g) | 14.4 oz (403 g) | 19.2 oz (544 g) | 24 oz (680 g) | 28.8 oz (816 g) |
| Turkey Necks | 1.6 oz (45 g) fresh or 0.32 oz (9 g) dry | 3.2 oz (90 g) fresh or 0.64 oz (18 g) dry | 4.8 oz (134 g) fresh or 0.96 oz (27 g) dry | 6.4 oz (179 g) fresh or 1.28 oz (36 g) dry | 8 oz (224 g) fresh or 1.6 oz (45 g) dry | 9.6 oz (269 g) fresh or 1.92 oz (54 g) dry |
| Pork Liver | 0.4 oz (11 g) fresh or 0.08 oz (2 g) dry | 0.8 oz (22 g) fresh or 0.16 oz (4 g) dry | 1.2 oz (34 g) fresh or 0.24 oz (7 g) dry | 1.6 oz (45 g) fresh or 0.32 oz (9 g) dry | 2 oz (56 g) fresh or 0.4 oz (11 g) dry | 2.4 oz (67 g) fresh or 0.48 oz (13 g) dry |
| Pork Kidney | 0.4 oz (11 g) fresh or 0.08 oz (2 g) dry | 0.8 oz (22 g) fresh or 0.16 oz (4 g) dry | 1.2 oz (34 g) fresh or 0.24 oz (7 g) dry | 1.6 oz (45 g) fresh or 0.32 oz (9 g) dry | 2 oz (56 g) fresh or 0.4 oz (11 g) dry | 2.4 oz (67 g) fresh or 0.48 oz (13 g) dry |
| Blue Mussels | 0.4 oz (11 g) fresh or 0.08 oz (2 g) dry | 0.8 oz (22 g) fresh or 0.16 oz (4 g) dry | 1.2 oz (34 g) fresh or 0.24 oz (7 g) dry | 1.6 oz (45 g) fresh or 0.32 oz (9 g) dry | 2 oz (56 g) fresh or 0.4 oz (11 g) dry | 2.4 oz (67 g) fresh or 0.48 oz (13 g) dry |
| Bone Broth | 1 oz (28 g) | 2 oz (56 g) | 3 oz (84 g) | 4 oz (112 g) | 5 oz (140 g) | 6 oz (168 g) |
| Pumpkin | 0.68 oz (19 g) | 1.36 oz (38 g) | 2.04 oz (57 g) | 2.72 oz (76 g) | 3.4 oz (95 g) | 4.08 oz (114 g) |
| Apple | 0.2 oz (6 g) | 0.4 oz (11 g) | 0.6 oz (17 g) | 0.8 oz (22 g) | 1 oz (28 g) | 1.2 oz (34 g) |
| Egg | 1 | 1 | 2 | 2 | 2 | 3 |
| Raw Goat Milk Kefir | ½ tbsp (8 ml) | 1 tbsp (15 ml) | 1 tbsp (15 ml) | 2 tbsp (30 ml) | 2 tbsp (30 ml) | 2 tbsp (30 ml) |

# GOOD DOG BURGER

Many popular raw dog food brands utilize a patty form for their food, so we thought we'd give it a go for our gently cooked recipes. These balanced burgers do involve grinding the meat, so if you don't have a grinder, this recipe will also work well in stew form, rather than as a burger. To make things even easier, you can measure out each patty to be the exact amount of food your dog needs per meal.

Ground beef (12 oz [336 g])

Beef liver (1 oz [28 g] fresh or 0.2 oz [6 g] dry)

Pork kidney (1 oz [28 g] fresh or 0.2 oz [6 g] dry)

Sweet potato (0.7 oz [20 g])

Pineapple (0.5 oz [14 g])

Sardines (1 oz [28 g] fresh or 0.2 oz [6 g] dry)

Oysters (1 oz [28 g] fresh or 0.2 oz [6 g] dry)

Spinach (1 oz [28 g])

Egg (1)

Beef short ribs (4 oz [112 g] fresh or 0.8 oz [22 g] dry) (not cooked with the rest)

In a large-sized mixing bowl, add the ground beef.

Grind the beef liver, pork kidney, sweet potato, pineapple, sardines and oysters into the same bowl.

With a spoon, stir in the spinach and egg until the mixture is fully combined.

Form into patties and cook in a pan over medium heat until fully cooked through, about 3 to 4 minutes per side.

Serve the burgers along with the beef short ribs on the side (beef short ribs are not cooked like the rest; see page 107 for air-drying bones).

Storage: We recommend storing any of your dog's meals in airtight containers in the fridge or freezer. Meals will generally last 2 to 4 days in the fridge and 3 to 4 months in the freezer.

Dosage: If your dog does not weigh one of the weights on the next page, see page 58 to determine your dog's daily food requirement based on their exact weight.

## Proportions by Weight

| | 20 lb (9 kg) | 40 lb (18 kg) | 60 lb (27 kg) | 80 lb (36 kg) | 100 lb (45 kg) | 120 lb (54.5 kg) |
|---|---|---|---|---|---|---|
| Ground Beef | 4.8 oz (134 g) | 9.6 oz (269 g) | 14.4 oz (403 g) | 19.2 oz (544 g) | 24 oz (680 g) | 28.8 oz (816 g) |
| Beef Liver | 0.4 oz (11 g) fresh or 0.08 oz (2 g) dry | 0.8 oz (22 g) fresh or 0.16 oz (4 g) dry | 1.2 oz (34 g) fresh or 0.24 oz (7 g) dry | 1.6 oz (45 g) fresh or 0.32 oz (9 g) dry | 2 oz (56 g) fresh or 0.4 oz (11 g) dry | 2.4 oz (67 g) fresh or 0.48 oz (13 g) dry |
| Pork Kidney | 0.4 oz (11 g) fresh or 0.08 oz (2 g) dry | 0.8 oz (22 g) fresh or 0.16 oz (4 g) dry | 1.2 oz (34 g) fresh or 0.24 oz (7 g) dry | 1.6 oz (45 g) fresh or 0.32 oz (9 g) dry | 2 oz (56 g) fresh or 0.4 oz (11 g) dry | 2.4 oz (67 g) fresh or 0.48 oz (13 g) dry |
| Sweet Potato | 0.28 oz (8 g) | 0.56 (16 g) | 0.84 oz (24 g) | 1.12 oz (31 g) | 1.4 oz (39 g) | 1.68 oz (47 g) |
| Pineapple | 0.2 oz (6 g) | 0.4 oz (11 g) | 0.6 oz (17 g) | 0.8 oz (22 g) | 1 oz (28 g) | 1.2 oz (34 g) |
| Sardines | 0.4 oz (11 g) fresh or 0.08 oz (2 g) dry | 0.8 oz (22 g) fresh or 0.16 oz (4 g) dry | 1.2 oz (34 g) fresh or 0.24 oz (7 g) dry | 1.6 oz (45 g) fresh or 0.32 oz (9 g) dry | 2 oz (56 g) fresh or 0.4 oz (11 g) dry | 2.4 oz (67 g) fresh or 0.48 oz (13 g) dry |
| Oysters | 0.4 oz (11 g) fresh or 0.08 oz (2 g) dry | 0.8 oz (22 g) fresh or 0.16 oz (4 g) dry | 1.2 oz (34 g) fresh or 0.24 oz (7 g) dry | 1.6 oz (45 g) fresh or 0.32 oz (9 g) dry | 2 oz (56 g) fresh or 0.4 oz (11 g) dry | 2.4 oz (67 g) fresh or 0.48 oz (13 g) dry |
| Spinach | 0.4 oz (11 g) | 0.8 oz (22 g) | 1.2 oz (34 g) | 1.6 oz (45 g) | 2 oz (56 g) | 2.4 oz (67 g) |
| Egg | 1 | 1 | 2 | 2 | 2 | 3 |
| Short Ribs | 1.6 oz (45 g) fresh or 0.32 oz (9 g) dry | 3.2 oz (90 g) fresh or 0.64 oz (18 g) dry | 4.8 oz (134 g) fresh or 0.96 oz (27 g) dry | 6.4 oz (179 g) fresh or 1.28 oz (36 g) dry | 8 oz (224 g) fresh or 1.6 oz (45 g) dry | 9.6 oz (269 g) fresh or 1.92 oz (54 g) dry |

# EGGY BREAKFAST HASH

**Eggy breakfast hash is one of our favorite human breakfasts (with a few different ingredients, of course). Eggs are considered a complete protein, making them a wonderful food for our canine companions. The addition of tahini is a great source of vitamin E, and this is a meal our dogs are particularly fond of.**

Chicken gizzards (9.3 oz [260 g])

Chicken liver (1 oz [28 g] fresh or 0.2 oz [6 g] dry)

Pork kidney (1 oz [28 g] fresh or 0.2 oz [6 g] dry)

Asparagus (0.5 oz [14 g])

Spinach (1.7 oz [48 g])

Sardines (1 oz [28 g] fresh or 0.2 oz 6 g] dry)

1–2 cups (240–480 ml) water or bone broth (page 121)

Eggs (2)

Raw goat milk (1 tbsp [15 ml])

Tahini (1 tbsp [14 g])

Wheat germ oil (2 tsp [10 ml])

Chicken feet (6.7 oz [188 g] fresh or 1.34 oz [38 g] dry) (not cooked with the rest)

NOTE: While boiling, add more water or bone broth as needed, but make sure the water is pretty much evaporated by the time the meat is done cooking.

Finely chop the chicken gizzards, chicken liver, pork kidney and asparagus (not required, but recommended for dogs new to these foods and for small dogs).

In a cold pan, add the chicken gizzards, chicken liver, kidney, asparagus, spinach, sardines and water or bone broth.

Place over high heat and bring the mixture to a boil. Boil until all the meat is cooked through, the water is fully evaporated and the veggies are fork tender, about 10 to 15 minutes.

Lower the heat to medium, crack in the eggs and scramble until cooked through, about 1 to 2 minutes.

Transfer to the bowl, drizzle the goat milk, tahini and wheat germ oil on top and give the chicken feet raw or gently air-dried (page 107) on the side.

Storage: We recommend storing any of your dog's meals in airtight containers in the fridge or freezer. Meals will generally last 2 to 4 days in the fridge and 3 to 4 months in the freezer.

Dosage: If your dog does not weigh one of the weights on the next page, see page 58 to determine your dog's daily food requirement based on their exact weight.

## Proportions by Weight

| | 20 lb (9 kg) | 40 lb (18 kg) | 60 lb (27 kg) | 80 lb (36 kg) | 100 lb (45 kg) | 120 lb (54.5 kg) |
|---|---|---|---|---|---|---|
| Chicken Gizzards | 3.72 oz (104 g) | 7.44 oz (208 g) | 11.16 oz (313 g) | 14.88 oz (417 g) | 18.6 oz (521 g) | 22.32 oz (625 g) |
| Chicken Liver | 0.4 oz (11 g) fresh or 0.08 oz (2 g) dry | 0.8 oz (22 g) fresh or 0.16 oz (4 g) dry | 1.2 oz (34 g) fresh or 0.24 oz (7 g) dry | 1.6 oz (45 g) fresh or 0.32 oz (9 g) dry | 2 oz (56 g) fresh or 0.4 oz (11 g) dry | 2.4 oz (67 g) fresh or 0.48 oz (13 g) dry |
| Pork Kidney | 0.4 oz (11 g) fresh or 0.08 oz (2 g) dry | 0.8 oz (22 g) fresh or 0.16 oz (4 g) dry | 1.2 oz (34 g) fresh or 0.24 oz (7 g) dry | 1.6 oz (45 g) fresh or 0.32 oz (9 g) dry | 2 oz (56 g) fresh or 0.4 oz (11 g) dry | 2.4 oz (67 g) fresh or 0.48 oz (13 g) dry |
| Asparagus | 0.2 oz (6 g) | 0.4 oz (11 g) | 0.6 oz (17 g) | 0.8 oz (22 g) | 1 oz (28 g) | 1.2 oz (34 g) |
| Spinach | 0.68 oz (19 g) | 1.36 oz (38 g) | 2.04 oz (57 g) | 2.72 oz (76 g) | 3.4 oz (95 g) | 4.08 oz (114 g) |
| Sardines | 0.4 oz (11 g) fresh or 0.08 oz (2 g) dry | 0.8 oz (22 g) fresh or 0.16 oz (4 g) dry | 1.2 oz (34 g) fresh or 0.24 oz (7 g) dry | 1.6 oz (45 g) fresh or 0.32 oz (9 g) dry | 2 oz (56 g) fresh or 0.4 oz (11 g) dry | 2.4 oz (67 g) fresh or 0.48 oz (13 g) dry |
| Water or Bone Broth | 1–2 cups (240–480 ml) | 1–2 cups (240–480 ml) | 1–2 cups (240–480 ml) | 1–2 cups (240–480 ml) | 1–2 cups (240–480 ml) | 1–2 cups (240–480 ml) |
| Eggs | 2 | 2 | 4 | 4 | 4 | 6 |
| Goat Milk | ½ tbsp (8 ml) | 1 tbsp (15 ml) | 1 tbsp (15 ml) | 2 tbsp (30 ml) | 2 tbsp (30 ml) | 2 tbsp (30 ml) |
| Tahini | ½ tbsp (7 g) | 1 tbsp (14 g) | 1 tbsp (14 g) | 2 tbsp (28 g) | 2 tbsp (28 g) | 2 tbsp (28 g) |
| Wheat Germ Oil | 1 tsp (5 ml) | 2 tsp (10 ml) | 2 tsp (10 ml) | 4 tsp (20 ml) | 4 tsp (20 ml) | 4 tsp (20 ml) |
| Chicken Feet | 2.68 oz (75 g) fresh or 0.54 oz (15 g) dry | 5.36 oz (150 g) fresh or 1.07 oz (30 g) dry | 8.04 oz (225 g) fresh or 1.61 oz (45 g) dry | 10.72 oz (300 g) fresh or 2.14 oz (60 g) dry | 13.4 oz (375 g) fresh or 2.68 oz (75 g) dry | 16.08 oz (450 g) fresh or 3.22 oz (90 g) dry |

The Modern Dog Parent Handbook

# TREATS

## ORGAN CHIPS

It's been observed in many wild carnivores that, after they take down an animal, they tend to go for the organ meat first, particularly the liver. This is because something hardwired in them knows that the organs are the most nutrient-dense parts of an animal. Your domesticated dog is no different, as they're sure to go crazy for these organ treats. This is also a great way to introduce kibble-fed dogs to organ meat, as dogs who have eaten one food most of their life tend to be pickier and not like the slimy and chewy texture of raw organs.

Makes about 1 oz (28 g)

5 oz (140 g) beef liver
1 tsp sesame seeds
1 tsp hemp hearts

Preheat the oven to 150°F (66°C). Line a baking sheet with parchment paper.

Puree the beef liver in a blender or food processor until it's completely smooth, or cut the liver into very thin slices.

Spread the organ mix or slices evenly onto the prepared baking sheet in as thin a layer as possible; we generally shoot for about ¼ inch (6 mm) thick of puree.

Sprinkle the sesame seeds and hemp hearts over the organ mix and bake for 4 to 8 hours or until the mixture is completely dried out. Let it cool to room temperature before serving.

Storage: Break into pieces and store in an airtight container for up to 2 months.

Dosage: Liver should only account for about 5 percent of your dog's overall diet, so use it sparingly.

# SKIN AND COAT SMOOTHIE TREATS

These treats are packed with omega-3s and probiotics, which can support a healthy immune system, diversify gut bacteria, generate healthier skin and coat, improve brain function and aid mobility. Omega-3s are fatty acids that we try to include in our dog's diet every single day. Whether it be these smoothie treats, other oily fish or even flaxseed, they're essential for a healthy dog to function properly and should be a staple in your dog's life.

Makes 18 to 28 treats

4 oz (120 ml) cow or goat milk kefir (unpasteurized is preferred over pasteurized kefir found in most supermarkets)

½ cup (120 ml) water

1 (4-oz [112-g]) can sardines in water (no salt added)

2 tbsp (30 ml) coconut oil

2 raw eggs

1 tbsp (8 g) spirulina powder

Combine all the ingredients in a blender or food processor and blend until the mixture is smooth.

Pour the mixture into your desired treat molds or ice cube trays.

Freeze them overnight and feed as treats or with meals.

Storage: Store these in the freezer for up to 1 month.

# HIP AND JOINT SMOOTHIE TREATS

As dogs age, one of the first signs you'll notice is decreased mobility. This can be brought on by a multitude of reasons, but one of the most common is inflammation. Inflammation decreases mobility, stiffens joints and can cause pain for your pup. These smoothie treats have a few anti-inflammatory ingredients, as well as some collagen that can really help them loosen up and provide some youthful energy!

Makes 18 to 28 treats

1 cup (240 ml) bone broth (page 121)

1 tbsp (14 g) golden paste (page 116)

2 raw eggs

Combine all the ingredients in a blender or food processor and blend until the mixture is smooth.

Pour the mixture into your desired treat molds or ice cube trays.

Freeze them overnight and feed as treats or with meals.

Storage: Store these in the freezer for up to 1 month.

# CANCER-FIGHTING SMOOTHIE TREATS

**Did you know that 50 percent of the dogs that pass away over the age of 10 do so because of some form of cancer? Providing your dog with antioxidant-rich foods can potentially lower their risk of developing cancer and even improve symptoms in pups currently battling cancer.**

Makes 18 to 28 treats

1 cup (240 ml) coconut water

¼ cup (37 g) blueberries

¼ cup (37 g) blackberries

¼ cup (32 g) carrot

2 tbsp (16 g) mushroom powder (page 119)

Combine all the ingredients in a blender or food processor and blend until the mixture is smooth.

Pour the mixture into your desired treat molds or ice cube trays.

Freeze them overnight and feed as treats or with meals.

Storage: Store these in the freezer for up to 1 month.

# GREEN BANANA TRAINING TREATS

Green bananas naturally have less sugar than their ripened future selves, making them a wonderful, healthy option for dogs. By dehydrating green bananas, you not only take away their stickiness, but you also turn them into a dry, crunchy treat that's perfect for walks or regular training. When we used to go to puppy class with our dogs, we tried wet treats in our treat pouch a couple of times and, let's just say, it did not work out. You won't have that issue with these! Green bananas are just what the name implies—unripe bananas—and are not to be confused with plantains.

Makes 30 to 60 treats

4 unripe (or green) bananas

Preheat the oven to 200°F (93°C).

Peel the bananas and cut them into your desired treat size.

Place the bananas on a wire rack and bake them for 6 to 8 hours or until they're completely dried out and crispy.

Feed as treats during training.

Storage: Store in an airtight container in a dark, cool place for 2 to 3 months.

# AIR-DRIED BEEF JERKY

We love air-dried meat treats because they don't add a ton of extra stuff to your dog's diet and they're single ingredient, so there are no preservatives or artificial ingredients. These beef jerky treats can be replaced with any ground meat, though you may have different drying times depending on what you choose.

Makes 3 to 4 oz
(84 to 112 g)

16 oz (454 g) ground beef

Preheat the oven or dehydrator to 150°F (66°C). Line a baking sheet with parchment paper.

Spread the ground beef on the prepared baking sheet until it's ¼ inch (6 mm) thick.

Dehydrate the ground beef for 10 to 15 hours, or until it's completely dried out and breaks apart like bark.

Storage: Store these in an airtight container for 1 to 2 months.

# CHAMOMILE CALMING BISCUITS

**These tasty treats are made with wonderful ingredients, such as chamomile, which is known for its soothing and calming effects. Whether your furry friend is feeling anxious, stressed or just in need of a little relaxation, these biscuits are the perfect solution.**

Makes 30 to 60 treats

¼ cup (8 g) dried chamomile

2 eggs

¼ cup (60 ml) bone broth (page 121)

3 tbsp (45 ml) melted coconut oil

2½ cups (313 g) oat flour

Preheat the oven to 325°F (165°C). Line a baking sheet with parchment paper.

In a large-sized mixing bowl, combine the chamomile, eggs, bone broth and coconut oil. Stir the ingredients together until they are well combined. Add the oat flour to the mixing bowl and stir until all of the ingredients are fully incorporated.

Using your hands or a spatula, flatten the dough until it is of uniform thickness (the thinner the dough is, the quicker the biscuits will cook). Use a cookie cutter or cut out shapes by hand. Transfer the cut-out dough to the prepared baking sheet.

Bake for 30 minutes, or until the biscuits are fully baked. Allow them to cool before storing in an airtight container.

Storage: Store these in an airtight container for up to 2 months.

NOTE: The dough may seem dry at first, but keep working it and it should firm up into a ball. If it's still too dry and crumbly, add an additional 1 tbsp (15 ml) of bone broth or water at a time until it comes together.

# SWEET POTATO CRISPS

Sweet potatoes are a fantastic vegetable to include in your dog's diet. They support the immune system and brain function and are usually a welcomed treat by even the pickiest of dogs. These crisps are great to take on the road or when you're traveling and will be sure to provide you with some satisfying sounds because of how crunchy they are.

Makes 10 to 15 treats

1 large sweet potato

Preheat the oven or dehydrator to 175°F (80°C).

Wash the sweet potato.

Cut the sweet potato into chip-size slices, as thin as you can get them. The thinner they are, the faster they will dry out. A mandoline is the ideal tool for this.

Spread the wedges evenly across a wire rack and dehydrate them for 4 to 8 hours, or until they're completely dried out.

Storage: Store these in an airtight container for 2 to 3 months.

# AIR-DRIED CHICKEN FEET

Chicken feet are a fantastic source of collagen and calcium; chewing on raw or air-dried meaty bones can do wonders for your dog's dental health. Dental disease is far less common in the wild because of the constant chewing of raw meaty bones by carnivores like wolves and dingoes. These chicken feet remove the raw aspect and allow you to store them at room temperature for several weeks!

Makes 6 to 7 oz
(168 to 196 g)

2 lb (907 g) chicken feet

Preheat the oven or dehydrator to 160°F (70°C).

Place the chicken feet on a wire rack, far enough apart that they are not touching.

Dehydrate them for 24 to 48 hours, or until they are completely dried out and no longer bend.

Storage: Store these in an airtight container for 1 to 2 months.

## Things to note about feeding non-raw bones

- All bones have a risk of splintering, even raw bones; the higher the heat used for cooking, the higher the chance of splintering.
- Raw and gently air-dried bones dried at or below 160°F (70°C) have the least chance of splintering.
- Bones cooked above 160°F (70°C) should never be fed to dogs. This includes smoked, boiled, roasted or otherwise high-heat cooked bones.

# SNACKS

Snacks are an area many dog parents have yet to discover. It's not quite a treat because you can't really use it for training or take it on the go, and it's certainly not a meal because it isn't balanced, but it is a nice in between to make for your dog during lunchtime or midafternoon. Sometimes, our dogs will vomit if they go too long without eating, so we give them a snack like the ones in this section to tide them over if mealtime is a little late.

## BERRY DELICIOUS OVERNIGHT OATS

**Our overnight oats recipe is packed with wholesome ingredients like rolled oats, yogurt and berries, and it's easy to make. Simply mix the ingredients together and let them sit in the fridge overnight. In the morning, your dog will be able to enjoy a tasty and nutritious snack.**

Makes 1 to 3 servings for a 30- to 50-lb (13.6- to 22.7-kg) dog

½ cup (45 g) rolled oats

2 tbsp (30 ml) water, plus more as needed

½ cup (120 ml) unsweetened yogurt

½ cup (74 g) fresh or frozen berries (such as blueberries, raspberries or blackberries)

½ tsp ground cinnamon

1½ tsp (5 g) ground flaxseed

In a medium-sized bowl, combine the oats, water, yogurt, berries, cinnamon and flaxseed. Stir the mixture until everything is well combined.

Cover the bowl with plastic wrap or a lid and refrigerate overnight.

In the morning, remove the bowl from the refrigerator and stir the mixture well. If the oats are too thick, you can add a splash of water to loosen them up.

Serve the desired amount as a treat or with food.

Storage: Store in an airtight container in the refrigerator for up to a week.

# SWEET POTATO CHIPS AND GUAC

I know what you're thinking. "Guac?! Avocados are not safe for dogs!" We thought the exact same thing when we first started this journey, only to find out some very surprising things! The study that claims avocados are toxic was based on feeding dogs the flesh, skin, leaves and other parts of the avocado that are most definitely toxic. New studies show that dogs who only ate the flesh showed no adverse health effects or changes, even when fed avocados at 18 percent of their overall diet! Just as humans can eat peaches with toxic pits in them, dogs can safely eat avocados as long as they don't consume the skin, leaves, stems or pits.

Makes 4 servings for a 30- to 50-lb (13.6- to 22.7-kg) dog

1 large sweet potato

1 tbsp (15 ml) avocado oil

1 tsp turmeric

1 tsp cinnamon

½ apple

1 large avocado, peeled and pitted

1 tbsp (2 g) dried parsley

Preheat the oven to 400°F (200°C). Line a baking sheet with parchment paper.

Cut the sweet potato into chip-size slices about ½ inch (1.3 cm) thick.

In a large-sized bowl, combine the sweet potato wedges, avocado oil, turmeric and cinnamon. Toss until the sweet potato is evenly coated with the oil and spices.

Place the sweet potatoes on the prepared baking sheet and bake for 20 to 25 minutes, or until fork tender. Allow to cool.

While the sweet potatoes bake, core and finely dice the apple.

Mash the avocado flesh in a bowl and combine with the diced apple and parsley.

Serve by dipping the potato wedges into the guacamole.

# NO-BAKE TAHINI OAT BALLS

**This recipe is packed with ingredients to support healthy skin and coats, like rolled oats, ground flaxseed and cinnamon. A dash of cinnamon also adds an anti-inflammatory touch, and the snacks are rolled into bite-size balls and coated in coconut shavings for added texture.**

Makes 10 to 20 balls

1 cup (90 g) rolled oats

¼ cup (42 g) ground flaxseed

½ cup (120 g) tahini

½ tsp ground cinnamon

½ cup (40 g) coconut shavings (100 percent coconut, not baker's coconut with added sugar)

In a medium-sized bowl, combine the rolled oats, flaxseed, tahini and cinnamon. Stir until everything is well combined and a dough-like consistency is formed.

Using your hands, roll the dough into bite-size balls.

Place the coconut shavings in a shallow dish. Roll each ball in the coconut shavings until it is evenly coated.

Place the balls on a plate or baking sheet and refrigerate for at least 30 minutes, or until firm.

Once the balls are firm, remove them from the refrigerator and serve them to your dog as a tasty and nutritious snack (1 to 3 per day, depending on the size of your dog).

Storage: Store these in an airtight container in the refrigerator for up to a week.

# PUP PARFAITS

These tasty treats are made with all-natural ingredients, including yogurt, strawberries, kiwis and our calming biscuits (page 103). Yogurt is a low-lactose dairy product that is full of probiotics, which are great for supporting your dog's gut health. The fresh strawberries and kiwi add a burst of flavor and a dose of antioxidants to support your dog's overall health and well-being.

Makes 1 to 3 servings for a 30- to 50-lb (13.6- to 22.7-kg) dog

2 strawberries, hulled

1 kiwi, peeled

1–2 calming biscuits (page 103) or your pup's favorite baked biscuit treat

¼ cup (60 ml) plain yogurt

Cut the strawberries and kiwi into bite-size pieces.

Crumble the calming biscuit treat and set it aside.

In a jar or small-sized bowl, add a layer of yogurt, followed by a layer of fresh strawberry and kiwi pieces.

Spread another layer of yogurt on the fruit, and then sprinkle the calming biscuit treat on top.

Chill the parfait until ready to serve.

Storage: Store in an airtight container in the refrigerator for up to a week.

# SUPPLEMENTS AND SUPERFOODS

## GOLDEN PASTE

Turmeric has long been used in many Asian countries for its anti-inflammatory properties, which is exactly why people include it to make golden paste. We love to mix golden paste into our dog's food, use it as a topper on lick mats and mix it into smoothie treats like you saw earlier in this book. This is a great supplement for all dogs, but start small to make sure it sits well before integrating this into your dog's regular diet. Once you know your dog does well on it, you can feed it daily or a few times per week.

Makes 10 to 16 oz (280 to 454 g)

1¼ cups (300 ml) water

½ cup (54 g) turmeric

⅓ cup (80 g) coconut oil

1 tbsp (6 g) freshly cracked black pepper

In a medium-sized pot, combine the water and turmeric, bring it to a gentle boil and stir. When the mixture has formed a sort of paste, remove it from the heat.

Let it cool slightly, but while it's still warm, transfer it to a glass jar and add the coconut oil and black pepper. Stir to combine.

Storage: Store in an airtight container in the fridge for up to 2 weeks, or freeze for up to 3 months.

Dosage: Give ½ teaspoon per 10 pounds (4.5 kg) of body weight per day.

# EGGSHELL CALCIUM POWDER

**Eggshells are about 95 percent calcium carbonate. Eggshell powder can be used as a calcium supplement in raw diets or for dogs who need an extra boost of calcium. All you need to do is save up your eggshells each time you crack a fresh egg, and you'll have a spice container full of this wonderful supplement in no time!**

Makes ¼ to ½ cup (24 to 48 g)

12 eggshells

Rinse the eggshells under cool water.

Line a bowl with paper towels, place the washed eggshells in the bowl and let them dry for about 4 hours.

Preheat the oven to 200°F (93°C). Line a baking sheet with parchment paper.

Spread the eggshells on the prepared baking sheet and bake for 10 to 20 minutes, or until completely dried out.

Transfer the eggshells to a blender, coffee grinder or food processor and process into a fine powder.

Storage: Store in an airtight container for up to 3 months.

Dosage: Give 1.25 g of powder per pound (455 g) of fresh food. Sprinkle the powder onto your dog's food as needed for extra calcium or as a calcium supplement in a homemade diet if your dog has trouble with bones. Keep in mind that if your dogs are fed a balanced diet that provides the calcium they need, they won't need extra calcium from this powder.

# MUSHROOM POWDER

Like avocados, mushrooms are another food long believed to be toxic to dogs; however, not only are human-safe mushrooms also safe for our companion animals, but they also offer some striking potential benefits. Certain mushrooms, like chaga and turkey tail, show potential cancer-fighting properties! As we stated in our Cancer-Fighting Smoothie Treat recipe (page 99), 50 percent of dogs over the age of 10 pass away from some form of cancer, so any foods showing potential cancer-fighting benefits are a wonderful addition to your dog's diet.

Makes ¼ to ½ cup (24 to 48 g)

16 oz (454 g) fresh turkey tail, chaga, reishi, lion's mane, cordyceps, shiitake and maitake mushrooms

Preheat the oven or dehydrator to 175°F (80°C).

Place the mushrooms on a wire rack, far enough apart that they are not touching.

Dehydrate for 2 to 6 hours, or until they are completely dried out. Drying time will depend on the type of mushroom and how thick or thin they are. Cutting mushrooms into thin slices will speed the drying process.

Place the dried mushrooms into a blender or food processor and blitz until they turn into a powder.

Storage: Store in an airtight container for up to 3 months.

Dosage: Sprinkle ½ teaspoon per 15 pounds (6.8 kg) of body weight on your dog's food.

# EVERYTHING BUT THE KITCHEN SINK BONE BROTH

**Bone broth will always be one of our all-time favorite "superfoods" for our dogs. It's packed with collagen, helps improve hydration and you can customize it based on what you have in the house, making it super easy and accessible. If you want to make a big batch and have it on hand, freeze it like you would the smoothie treats (page 98) and store it in the freezer.**

Makes about 2 quarts (2 L)

2–3 lb (908–1362 g) marrow-bones

¼ cup (60 ml) apple cider vinegar

3 cups (weight varies) chopped vegetables of your choice (we love broccoli, asparagus, mushrooms and carrots)

3 cloves garlic

3 tbsp (15 g) ground ginger

2 tbsp (14 g) turmeric

1 tsp black pepper

In a slow cooker, add the bones, apple cider vinegar and enough water to cover everything.

Cook on low for 24 hours.

With about 30 minutes to 1 hour left, add the vegetables, garlic, ginger, turmeric and pepper.

Once the broth is done cooking, strain it into heat-safe jars for storage.

Storage: Store bone broth in an airtight container in the fridge for up to a week, or in the freezer for 1 to 2 months.

Dosage: Give 1 ounce (30 ml) of bone broth per 20 pounds (9 kg) of body weight each day.

# Part Two

# ENRICHING YOUR DOG'S LIFE

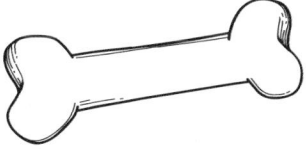

Chapter 7

# MENTAL ENRICHMENT

As a new pet parent, one of the first things you probably learned is how important physical exercise is, whether it be walks, playing fetch or going on hikes; most people know that a tired dog is a good dog and movement of almost any kind is beneficial to humans and animals alike. What you probably didn't learn is the fact that mental stimulation and mental exercise is, quite literally, just as important. Mental enrichment is any activity designed to improve and enhance your pet's mental state and exercise their brain. These activities encourage dogs to problem solve, learn new skills and become more confident.

Throughout the week, your mental enrichment as a human may consist of watching TV, reading books, having conversations with friends, going to dinner parties, trying new foods, meeting new people, going new places, etc. Chances are, if you are doing one or a few of these things, your life feels enriched. Now, imagine trying to get your source of enrichment from a 2-mile (1.2-km) jog every day, instead of from the aforementioned activities. It's not possible, because physical exercise doesn't do the same thing for us that social and mental enrichment does. The same thing applies to our pets. Going on a 2-mile (1.2-km) jog with your dog is a fantastic way to meet their physical exercise needs, but unless you are stopping to let them sniff regularly, they are getting little to no mental stimulation. The good news is, there are a multitude of ways to provide mental enrichment for your dog, making it very easy to find a method that will seamlessly integrate into your lifestyle.

## USES

There doesn't have to be any special occasion for you to provide mental enrichment for your dog. It can be a daily activity integrated into your regular schedule; it can replace meals or be an occasional treat. This is what we call casual enrichment. No goal whatsoever, other than to mentally stimulate your dog and give them something fun to do.

The other side of this is what we like to call functional enrichment. Functional enrichment is just what it sounds like: Providing enrichment in hopes of getting your dog to stay calm, perform a certain activity, have a distraction or make an experience easier. Here's an example. Our dog Banksy is not a big fan of being brushed. He turns into the Tasmanian devil and becomes almost impossible to corral. He sheds a ton, so not brushing is not an option for us. This is where functional enrichment comes into play. We generally provide a big chew, a lick mat or some other enrichment activity to get him to calm down, stay in one spot and allow us to get all of his brushing done. It works 100 percent of the time.

Other uses include going to the vet/groomer, car rides, baths at home, nail trims, ear cleanings, when guests come over, during fireworks or thunderstorms and many other situations yet to be discovered. Tools like lick mats (more on these later) often have styles with suction cups on the back, making them perfect for sticking to a window, wall or tub. Whether you provide casual or functional enrichment, it has so many benefits!

# BENEFITS

How does mental enrichment actually benefit your dog? In a few different ways. First, it can reduce stress and anxiety. Providing enrichment for your companion animal that encourages repeated licking or mental energy to figure something out releases endorphins in their brain, which can help regulate the nervous system and promote calmness. The excess saliva generated during licking-type enrichment activities can help improve digestion and gut health, as well as dental health because the saliva helps clean the tongue, teeth and gums. This type of enrichment is also very beneficial for senior dogs to help keep their mind active. It can fend off and even reverse the effects of doggy dementia. It's even extremely beneficial for puppies who have an abundance of energy that needs to be released.

If you do additional research on enrichment, a term you will most likely come across is *contrafreeloading*. Contrafreeloading occurs when an animal is offered a choice between free food or identical food that requires effort. Usually, the animal prefers the food that requires effort. Why? Because your dog wants to work for their food!

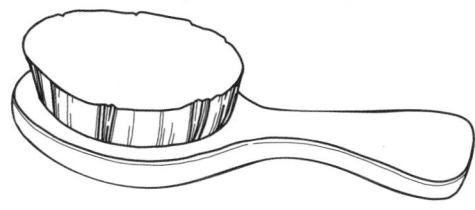

# TYPES OF ENRICHMENT

## Licking

As we mentioned earlier, repeated licking has many benefits, such as reducing stress and anxiety, burning excess energy and improving dental health through scraping of the tongue and increased saliva production.

A great beginner tool for licking enrichment is a lick mat. *Lick mat* is an extremely broad term used to describe enrichment activities that promote repeated licking by your dog. With lick mats, we generally like to start with a spreadable base or their regular food and top it with various treats and supplements (see page 139 for enrichment recipes). The DIY version of lick mats would be freezing the same foods onto a dish, inside a muffin tin or spread out on a silicone mat. While you may not get the same tongue-scraping benefits if the lick mat is smooth, it's still very enriching and mentally stimulating for your pets. Lick mats and flat eating surfaces are great for all breeds, even flat-nosed breeds, because they don't require your dog to fit their snout into a specific-size hole.

Another licking-style enrichment toy we use is the West Paw Toppl. It's a cup-shaped rubber toy designed to hold various treats, pet food or supplements. The reason we love this enrichment toy so much is because it is the only toy, in the history of all the toys that have ever entered the Francois household, that has never been chewed through. It's also much easier to handle and has a tendency to spill a lot less, because of the cup shape. You can even make them last longer or make them more challenging by connecting two Toppls together (one large and one small or one large and one extra-large).

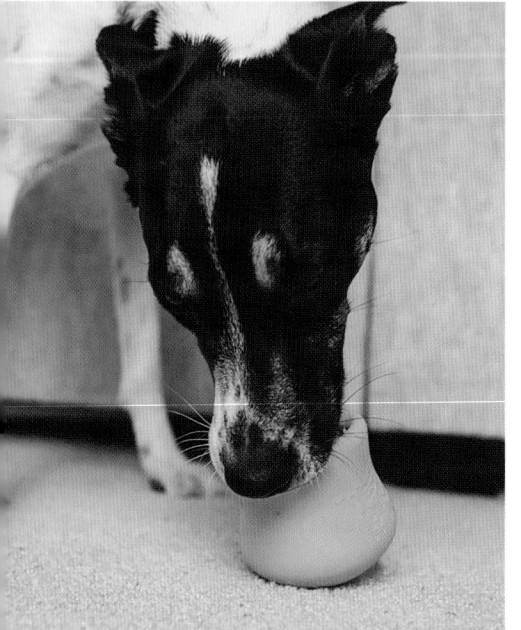

← West Paw Toppl

130

## Sniffing

Dogs perceive so much of their environment through their nose; it's one of, if not the most, powerful sense that they have. Not only do dogs have hundreds of millions of scent receptors as compared to humans' six million, but they also devote approximately 40 times more brain volume to decoding smells than we do, according to PetMD. This is why we encourage you to go on sniff walks, provide meals that require foraging and even spread food around your backyard or home for your dog to search for and find. It engages their mind, improves their brain function and provides them with endless entertainment, not to mention most of these methods are free or extremely inexpensive.

Let's talk sniff walks. Sniff walks are walks where your dog mostly leads you and they are able to sniff whatever they want (within reason). Be prepared for these walks to be much slower than a normal one. Sniff walks provide much more mental stimulation than regular walks, as your dog is able to freely make decisions on where they want to go and what they want to sniff. Normal walks are great and they have their place in the daily routines of millions of people, but they don't do much for your dog outside of physical exercise if they don't have an opportunity to explore.

## Foraging

Because dogs are natural-born scavengers, allowing them an outlet to forage provides them an opportunity to act on deep-rooted instincts. There are so many methods to provide foraging enrichment, but here are a few of our favorites.

First up, wobble toys. They are exactly what they sound like. They're egg-shaped toys that are generally hollow, allowing you to put dry treats or food inside. They also have a small opening for the treats to dispense as your dog pushes it and rolls it around. If you feed kibble, this is a great way to make mealtime more enriching and entice picky eaters to eat. It engages their prey and scavenging drive, which is very effective in tiring out your pup. The DIY version of wobble toys would be putting treats or food inside an empty (and clean) plastic bottle. Some bottles have really small openings, so using something like a Gatorade® bottle may be easier. (The smaller the hole, the more challenging!)

Next are snuffle mats. Snuffle mats are another way to ditch the food bowl and make mealtime more engaging. They're generally made of fabric and designed to hide dry food in, to mimic foraging in the wild. The DIY version of a snuffle mat would be laying out a towel, sprinkling dry food or treats all over it and rolling it up into a log so your pup has to open it up to get the food. For an added challenge, tie a knot in the towel; you'll be surprised at how smart they are! Another DIY snuffle mat method is to sprinkle their food or treats around your house and/or backyard. You can even feed complete meals this way! One last method is to gather a selection of nonedible household objects, such as a wooden spoon, ripped-up newspapers or dog toys, and place them in a shoebox. Sprinkle treats among the objects and encourage your dog to search for and find the treats hidden in the box.

← Snuffle mats

134

## Social Enrichment

*Social enrichment* is a term that refers to providing new and stimulating experiences for dogs to support their physical, mental and emotional well-being. This can include activities like playing with other dogs, exploring new environments and learning new skills and tricks. Other methods include dog parks (but not in the way that you think, more on that on page 149), dog-friendly stores and even group training sessions. Providing social enrichment for your dog has numerous benefits, such as improving their cognitive function, reducing boredom and destructive behavior and strengthening the bond between you and your pet. In addition, social enrichment can help prevent behavior problems and increase your dog's confidence and adaptability. Dogs are intelligent, social animals that need mental and physical stimulation to stay happy and healthy. By providing as many new experiences for your dog as possible, you can enrich their lives and ensure that they are getting the mental and physical exercise they need.

One other enrichment method that many people tend to overlook is observing. Observing, simply put, is allowing your dog to take in their current environment without you really asking for anything. Whether it's looking out the window or sitting at a bench in a park while other people and pets walk by, giving them a chance to observe and rewarding calm behavior will work their brain and strengthen the bond you share with them. In the beginning, it may be hard to get them to be still and simply observe, especially in public, but if you work at desensitizing them to new experiences, you have a much higher chance for success.

# RECIPES

These recipes are not designed for one specific tool like a lick mat, but instead can be used for multiple tools and even some of the DIY enrichment methods. The ingredients in each recipe can also be blended in a blender or food processor and used as food mix-ins or smoothie treats for dogs who are picky about any of the foods we have listed.

NOTE: It's important to always supervise your dog while they are using enrichment tools, such as toys, puzzles and lick mats. While these tools can provide valuable mental stimulation for your dog, they can also pose a choking hazard if your dog starts to chew on them. It's important to monitor your dog closely and intervene if they start to chew to prevent any potential choking incidents.

# BERRIES AND CREAM

This tasty treat is packed with antioxidants, vitamins and minerals; it is sure to be a hit with your furry friend! The combination of creamy kefir and fresh berries is a healthy and delicious way to add some excitement and fresh food to your dog's diet. This recipe can be used for lick mats or Toppls or made into smoothie treats (page 98).

Makes 1 serving for a 30- to 50-lb (13.6- to 22.7-kg) dog

¼ cup (60 ml) raw cow or goat milk kefir

A few blueberries

A few blackberries

A few raspberries

Pour the kefir onto the lick mat and spread it evenly so it reaches all four corners.

Place the berries on top.

Freeze for at least 2 to 3 hours.

Serve to your pup!

139

# THE MEAL REPLACEMENT

This recipe is essentially just making one of our raw recipes much more engaging for your dog. As with the rest of the meal recipes, make sure you're calculating how much food your dog should eat and not just relying on the amounts we use (remember, these amounts are for a 50-pound [22.7-kg] dog). To calculate how much food your dog needs in this recipe, use the equation on page 58 or the table on the next page.

Ground beef (12.6 oz [353 g])

Raw goat milk (1 tbsp [15 ml])

Chicken feet (3.4 oz [95 g] fresh or 0.68 oz [19 g] dry)

Beef liver (1 oz [28 g] fresh or 0.2 oz [6 g] dry)

Beef kidney (1 oz [28 g] fresh or 0.2 oz [6 g] dry)

Steamed red bell pepper (1.7 oz [48 g])

Blueberries (0.5 oz [14 g])

Sardines (1 oz [28 g] fresh or 0.2 oz [6 g] dry)

Green-lipped mussels (1 oz [28 g] fresh or 0.2 oz [6 g] dry)

Spread and smoosh the ground beef all over a lick mat of your choice.

Drizzle the goat milk on top of the ground beef.

Top with the rest of the ingredients (don't be afraid to stack it high if you need) and push them into the ground beef so they freeze together.

Freeze for at least 4 hours, ideally overnight.

Feed as a replacement for one day's worth of meals.

Storage: This will stay good in the freezer for about a week, but ideally should be fed 4 to 24 hours after preparing it.

Dosage: This recipe is an entire day's worth of food for a 50-pound (22.7-kg) dog.

## Proportions by Weight

| | 20 lb (9 kg) | 40 lb (18 kg) | 60 lb (27 kg) | 80 lb (36 kg) | 100 lb (45 kg) | 120 lb (54.5 kg) |
|---|---|---|---|---|---|---|
| Ground Beef | 5.04 oz (141 g) | 10.08 oz (282 g) | 15.12 oz (423 g) | 20.16 oz (572 g) | 25.2 oz (714 g) | 30.24 oz (857 g) |
| Goat Milk | ½ tbsp (8 ml) | 1 tbsp (15 ml) | 1 tbsp (15 ml) | 2 tbsp (30 ml) | 2 tbsp (30 ml) | 2 tbsp (30 ml) |
| Chicken Feet | 1.36 oz (38 g) fresh or 0.27 oz (8 g) dry | 2.72 oz (76 g) fresh or 0.54 oz (15 g) dry | 4.08 oz (114 g) fresh or 0.82 oz (23 g) dry | 5.44 oz (152 g) fresh or 1.09 oz (31 g) dry | 6.8 oz (190 g) fresh or 1.36 oz (38 g) dry | 8.16 oz (229 g) fresh or 1.63 oz (46 g) dry |
| Beef Liver | 0.4 oz (11 g) fresh or 0.08 oz (2 g) dry | 0.8 oz (22 g) fresh or 0.16 oz (4 g) dry | 1.2 oz (34 g) fresh or 0.24 oz (7 g) dry | 1.6 oz (45 g) fresh or 0.32 oz (9 g) dry | 2 oz (56 g) fresh or 0.4 oz (11 g) dry | 2.4 oz (67 g) fresh or 0.48 oz (13 g) dry |
| Beef Kidney | 0.4 oz (11 g) fresh or 0.08 oz (2 g) dry | 0.8 oz (22 g) fresh or 0.16 oz (4 g) dry | 1.2 oz (34 g) fresh or 0.24 oz (7 g) dry | 1.6 oz (45 g) fresh or 0.32 oz (9 g) dry | 2 oz (56 g) fresh or 0.4 oz (11 g) dry | 2.4 oz (67 g) fresh or 0.48 oz (13 g) dry |
| Bell Pepper | 0.68 oz (19 g) | 1.36 oz (38 g) | 2.04 oz (57 g) | 2.72 oz (76 g) | 3.4 oz (95 g) | 4.08 oz (114 g) |
| Blueberries | 0.2 oz (6 g) | 0.4 oz (11 g) | 0.6 oz (17 g) | 0.8 oz (22 g) | 1 oz (28 g) | 1.2 oz (34 g) |
| Sardines | 0.4 oz (11 g) fresh or 0.08 oz (2 g) dry | 0.8 oz (22 g) fresh or 0.16 oz (4 g) dry | 1.2 oz (34 g) fresh or 0.24 oz (7 g) dry | 1.6 oz (45 g) fresh or 0.32 oz (9 g) dry | 2 oz (56 g) fresh or 0.4 oz (11 g) dry | 2.4 oz (67 g) fresh or 0.48 oz (13 g) dry |
| Mussels | 0.4 oz (11 g) fresh or 0.08 oz (2 g) dry | 0.8 oz (22 g) fresh or 0.16 oz (4 g) dry | 1.2 oz (34 g) fresh or 0.24 oz (7 g) dry | 1.6 oz (45 g) fresh or 0.32 oz (9 g) dry | 2 oz (56 g) fresh or 0.4 oz (11 g) dry | 2.4 oz (67 g) fresh or 0.48 oz (13 g) dry |

# THE DREAMY TAHINI

Introducing a dreamy lick mat recipe! This delicious and nutritious treat is made with three simple ingredients: tahini, strawberries and dried parsley. The creamy tahini provides a rich and satisfying base as well as a boost of vitamin E, while the fresh strawberries add a pop of color and antioxidants. The dried parsley adds a hint of freshness, which can aid bad breath, making this lick mat a treat that both you and your dog will love.

Makes 1 serving for a 30- to 50-lb (13.6- to 22.7-kg) dog

3 tbsp (45 g) tahini
A few chopped strawberries
A sprinkle of dried parsley

Pour the tahini onto a lick mat and spread it evenly so it reaches all four corners.

Smoosh the chopped strawberries into the tahini and sprinkle with the dried parsley.

Freeze for at least 2 to 3 hours.

Serve to your pup!

# FOR GUT HEALTH

This lick mat is super simple with all-natural ingredients, including kefir and pumpkin, which are both packed with benefits for your furry friend. Kefir is full of probiotics, which are great for supporting your dog's gut health. Pumpkin, on the other hand, is a great source of fiber, which can help relieve both constipation and diarrhea.

Makes 1 serving for a 30- to 50-lb (13.6- to 22.7-kg) dog

¼ cup (60 ml) raw cow or goat's milk kefir

2 tbsp (30 g) canned pumpkin

1 tbsp (9 g) hemp hearts

Pour the kefir and pumpkin onto a lick mat and spread it evenly so it reaches all four corners.

Sprinkle the hemp hearts all over the mat.

Freeze for at least 2 to 3 hours.

Serve to your pup!

## Chapter 8

# REMOVING STRESSORS FROM YOUR DOG'S LIFE

## YOUR STRESS

Thousands of years ago, when dogs and humans first began interacting, any stress that we or our canine companions felt was a result of physical dangers in the outside world. These stressors included things like being chased by a predator or trying to bring down a large animal during a hunt. In today's world, most modern stressors include worries about money, keeping up with societal standards, work, safety and even access to basic modern amenities. While the stressors are much different than what they were thousands of years ago, what happens in our body physiologically when we feel stress is largely the same. According to the American Psychological Association, "When the body is stressed, the SNS (sympathetic nervous system) contributes to what is known as the 'fight or flight' response. The body shifts its energy resources toward fighting off a life threat, or fleeing from an enemy.

The SNS signals the adrenal glands to release hormones called adrenaline (epinephrine) and cortisol. These hormones, together with direct actions of autonomic nerves, cause the heart to beat faster, respiration rate to increase, blood vessels in the arms and legs to dilate, digestive process to change and glucose levels (sugar energy) in the bloodstream to increase to deal with the emergency." In short, whether the threat is a looming predator or an overdue bill, our body reacts the same because it cannot differentiate between the two. It's always preparing to fight or flee.

You're probably wondering why we are talking about human stress. The reality is that our stress, mental health and personality are all closely tied to that of our companion animals. Various studies have shown correlations in cortisol levels between pet parents and their dogs. This information isn't meant to scare you or make you think you are emotionally harming your dog, but instead to make you aware that your dog is much more attuned to your emotions than you may realize. Lina Roth, a professor at Linkoping University in Sweden and author of one of the aforementioned studies, states, "I don't think you should be anxious that, if you're stressed, you might harm your dog. Instead, your dog is a social support for you, and you are a social support for the dog." In our own lives, if either of us starts crying, our oldest dog, Harper, is instantly in our face trying to lick up our tears. So, while our dogs do feel and pick up on our emotions, the good news is there are many things we can do to mitigate our own stress and, in turn, our dog's stress.

**Ways to Manage Stress**

- 4-7-8 breathing (in for 4 seconds, hold for 7 seconds and exhale for 8 seconds)
- Yoga
- Meditation
- Eating a diverse array of nutrient-dense whole foods
- Engaging in regular exercise (bonus points if your walks/runs include your pup)
- Maintaining a healthy support system
- Getting plenty of sleep each night
- Standing in the sun
- Journaling
- Finding a creative outlet
- Therapy

We are in no way stress-reduction professionals; these are just some of the methods that have worked for us. If any of them sparks your interest, we encourage you to do more research on these techniques and how you can integrate them into your life.

# DOG-TO-DOG INTERACTION

In our opinion, one of the biggest myths perpetuated to dog parents is that socializing your dog means letting your dog interact with other, random dogs. Dog parks have become so prevalent that you can find at least one or more in most towns and cities. If you go to one of these dog parks, you're likely to find tons of dogs of all different shapes, sizes and backgrounds, along with pet parents who may not be paying enough attention, or any attention at all, to their dogs and what they are doing. Even if they are paying attention, most dog parks are huge, which makes it hard for pet parents to be close enough to react if something were to happen. Now, please don't think we are bashing pet parents who do this, because we used to do the exact same thing. Heck, we would even take a book to read while they ran around or would chat with other pet parents. You simply don't know what you don't know.

Because of the aforementioned ways dog parks are utilized, they become breeding grounds for injuries, fights, disease and increased reactivity in dogs. This is one area where most veterinarians, whether they are conventional or integrative, can agree: Dog parks are more harmful than beneficial and socialization can be achieved in safer ways. There is even a trend on social media where someone in a vet's office will ask the entire staff, "What is something you'll never do after working at a vet's office?" and a majority of the responses will include not taking their dogs to dog parks.

On the flip side, there are a few ways that you can use dog parks to your benefit. The first way is going when no one is there and leaving if someone shows up. Empty dog parks are a great way to give your dog ample room to run and sniff, which is physically and mentally enriching. This worked really well for us when we lived in a small town in Wyoming, as most of our dog parks were empty, especially in the winter.

If you don't have access to an empty dog park, you can still go to one, even if it's full, and train your dog from the outside. Get as close as you can to the fence of the dog park, while still being able to maintain your dog's attention (even if you have to use treats), and just teach calmness in the chaos. Other dogs are a huge stimulus, but teaching your dog to remain calm and pay attention to you in the presence of such stimuli will desensitize them, set you up with an extremely sociable dog and strengthen your bond. Another alternative is Sniffspot. Sniffspot is essentially the Airbnb of private, dog-safe land. They have an app where you can reserve your own space for a certain amount of time and you can see what amenities they have, such as agility equipment, pools or toys. These have become part of our weekly routine and we highly recommend checking out what Sniffspot has to offer in your area.

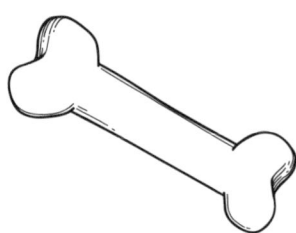

# TOXIC INGREDIENTS

In this section, we talk a lot about different foods and ingredients that could be potentially toxic. Please don't feel bad if you use or give some of these ingredients, as you can't avoid every single thing that is bad for you. Most of the substances aren't super harmful in small quantities, but when given or used over a long period of time, they can build up in a dog's system and cause issues.

## Artificial Colors

Ingestion of artificial colors such as Red 40, Yellow 5, Blue 2 and Yellow 6 can be potentially dangerous for a dog's health. These artificial colors are commonly found in a variety of processed and packaged foods and are used to enhance the color and appearance of pet food so it better appeals to pet parents. And if you didn't know, dogs can't see all of the same colors we can see, so any time a company is adding artificial colors to their products, they're doing it to trick you into buying it, not because it has any benefit to your dog.

Artificial colors have been linked to a variety of health issues in dogs. These include digestive problems such as vomiting and diarrhea, as well as more serious conditions like allergies and chronic disease. Ingestion of these artificial colors can also lead to a weakened immune system, making dogs more susceptible to illness and disease. Weakened immune systems are precursors to many chronic diseases such as cancer. Opt for foods without artificial colors that instead use natural colorings like annatto, paprika, beet juice and turmeric.

## Preservatives

BHA, BHT and ethoxyquin are synthetic preservatives commonly used in pet food and treats. There are many dangers associated with ingesting these preservatives, such as cancer, liver damage and allergic reactions. These dangers have been well documented by researchers and veterinarians. Because these preservatives are synthetic, they are not naturally occurring, and therefore a dog's body is not designed to consume them. Consuming small amounts may be harmless from the outside, but long-term ingestion by dogs who eat the same food with these ingredients every day can lead to a buildup of the synthetic preservatives, which can then lead to the aforementioned diseases.

Synthetic preservatives are also suspected of being endocrine disruptors. They can interfere with the way hormones work throughout the body, which will inevitably lead to health issues down the road. Opt for food and treats that use natural preservatives like vitamins C and E, rather than synthetic products.

## Fragrances

Fragrances, such as those found in candles, air fresheners, cleaning products, dog shampoo, certain essential oils and many other consumer goods can be harmful to dogs if they are inhaled or ingested. Dogs have a much more sensitive sense of smell than humans do, which means they can be easily overwhelmed by strong scents.

Inhaling fragrances can cause irritation to the respiratory system, leading to symptoms such as coughing, sneezing and difficulty breathing. In severe cases, exposure to fragrances can cause lung damage, seizures and even death. Many fragrances contain chemicals that can be toxic when ingested, such as alcohol and certain essential oils. Even small amounts of these substances can cause vomiting, diarrhea and other digestive issues in dogs.

It is important to be cautious when using fragrances around dogs. It is best to avoid using fragrances altogether, or to use them sparingly and in well-ventilated areas. If you must use fragrances, keep them out of reach of your dog and monitor your dog carefully for any signs of distress. If your dog shows any symptoms of respiratory or digestive distress, or is acting weird in any way after being exposed to fragrances, contact your veterinarian immediately.

## Cleaning Supplies

Household cleaning products can be dangerous for dogs if ingested or if they come into contact with the skin. Ingesting cleaning products can cause stomach and digestive issues, such as vomiting and diarrhea. In more severe cases, it can lead to organ damage and even death. In addition to the risks associated with ingestion, cleaning products can be harmful if they come into contact with a dog's skin. Some products, such as bleach, can cause irritation and redness. In more severe cases, it can lead to chemical burns and other serious injuries.

It's important to keep all cleaning products out of reach of dogs. This means storing them in a cabinet or closet that is securely closed and out of reach of curious noses. It's also a good idea to use natural cleaning products whenever possible. These products are less likely to contain harmful chemicals and are safer for use around pets.

In the event that a dog does come into contact with a cleaning product, it's important to act quickly. If the product has been ingested, it's best to call a veterinarian immediately. They will be able to provide advice on how to proceed and may need to see the dog for further treatment. If the cleaning product has come into contact with the skin, it's important to rinse the affected area with water and to contact a veterinarian if the dog shows any signs of discomfort or irritation.

## Lawn Care

Pesticides, insecticides and fertilizers are commonly used in households and gardens to control pests and promote plant growth. While these substances can be effective in achieving their intended purposes, they can also pose serious dangers to our canine friends. Ingestion of these substances can cause symptoms such as vomiting, diarrhea, tremors, seizures and even death. Inhaling the fumes from these chemicals can be harmful to your dog's respiratory system and overall well-being. Chronic exposure to these chemicals can weaken their immune system, making them more susceptible to illness and disease. It can also cause hormonal imbalances and reproductive problems.

It is important for you to take steps to protect your pets from the dangers of these substances. The first step is to carefully read and follow the instructions on the labels of these products. It is also important to keep dogs away from areas where these substances are being applied, and to thoroughly wash their paws after they have been in contact with treated areas. In addition to taking these precautions, you should consider using safer alternatives to pesticides, insecticides and fertilizers. There are many natural and organic options available that can be effective in controlling pests and promoting plant growth without posing a risk to your dog.

# FURTHERING YOUR KNOWLEDGE

## Social Media Accounts

- Rachel Fusaro (@rachelfusaro) Nutrition/Training
- Dr. Judy Morgan (@drjudymorgan) Holistic Veterinary Care/Nutrition
- Hahnbee Choi (@therawstorm) Raw Feeding
- Mariah (@pawsofprey) Raw Feeding
- Dr. Angie Krause (@boulderholisticvet) Holistic Veterinary Care/Nutrition
- Hannah (@dailydogfoodrecipes) Nutrition
- Kayla Kowalski (@kaylakowalskinutrition) Raw Feeding
- Taylor (@bindisbucketlist) Enrichment
- Feed Real Movement (@feedrealmovement) Raw Feeding
- Loving Dog Training (@lovingdogtrainingllc) R+ Dog Training
- Dr. Andrew Jones (@veterinarysecrets) Natural Pet Health
- Kerrie Norman (@situated_canine) R+ Dog Training
- Renee (@r.plus.dogs) R+ Dog Training
- Ginger and Kassidi (@gingers_naps) Antiracist Animal Advocacy
- Dr. Karen Becker (@drkarenbecker) Nutrition and Holistic Pet Care
- Rodney Habib (@rodneyhabib) Nutrition and Holistic Pet Care
- Perfectly Rawsome (@perfectlyrawsome) Raw Feeding and Nutrition
- Tia (@crimsonthecavapoo) Diversity and Inclusivity in the Pet Industry

## Sourcing

- thebkpets.com for all of our latest brand recommendations

## Books

- *Feeding Dogs: Dry or Raw? The Science Behind the Debate* by Dr. Conor Brady
- *The Spirit of Animal Healing* by Dr. Marty Goldstein
- *Big Kibble: The Hidden Dangers of the Pet Food Industry and How to Do Better by Our Dogs* by Shawn Buckley and Dr. Oscar Chavez
- *The Forever Dog* by Dr. Karen Becker and Rodney Habib
- *Yin & Yang Nutrition for Dogs* by Dr. Judy Morgan and Hue Grant
- *Raw Meaty Bones* by Dr. Tom Lonsdale
- *Give Your Dog a Bone* by Dr. Ian Billinghurst

# ACKNOWLEDGMENTS

First and foremost, we would like to thank our incredible community for all the support and love that you give us. Nothing we do, especially this book, would be possible without you.

Next we would like to thank everyone at the Page Street Publishing team, especially our editor, Marissa Giambelluca, for taking a chance on us and turning this idea into a reality, and our copyeditor, Karen Levy, for all her work on the manuscript.

Another thank you to Laurel, who captured all of the photos; they're everything we hoped for and more.

To Dr. Judy Morgan, thank you so much for not only writing the foreword for this book, but also for reviewing it to ensure we are providing the most accurate information possible. You do wonderful things for pets everywhere.

To our moms, you have supported us through this entire journey and stuck by us even when things seemed hard. You two did more for this book than you will ever realize and we cannot thank you enough.

To Francesca, our manager, you are an absolute angel. You do so much for the BK brand and help guide us to exactly where we are trying to go.

To Madison, our video editor, you have stuck with us from literally day one, have gone through all the ups and downs of ventures before this and yet you still ride with us. You are irreplaceable.

We couldn't have dreamt of a better team. We would like to thank all of our friends and family who have supported us from day one, no matter what dream we are pursuing. You know who you are and we are forever grateful. Lastly, we want to thank you, the reader. You are the reason we wrote this book and we truly hope it helps you improve the lives of your dogs at home.

# ABOUT THE AUTHORS

Bryce and Kenzie Francois are a devoted husband and wife team from Wyoming who share an immense passion for animals, leading them to commit their lives to supporting their longevity. The couple first crossed paths while participating in a social media internship for the University of Wyoming Athletics Department. They quickly formed a strong bond, collaborating on various content and video projects, which eventually led to the beginning of their romantic relationship in 2017.

Throughout the following years, Bryce and Kenzie welcomed three dogs into their family: Harper, Cooper and Banksy. Harper and Cooper are Australian Shepherd siblings from separate litters but with the same parentage. Banksy, a rescue dog from the harsh weather and blackouts Texas faced in 2021, is predominantly Husky, although his appearance may not immediately suggest it.

In 2021, influenced by several podcasts featuring Dr. Karen Becker and Rodney Habib, the couple began transitioning their dogs to a raw/gently cooked diet. The podcasts emphasized the evolutionary basis for dogs consuming raw diets and highlighted the relatively short history of kibble as a pet food source. This information led Bryce and Kenzie to question the prevalence of processed food pellets for pets. They shared their experiences with the community they established through their business, which had about 200k followers on TikTok at the time. As of December 2022, their community has grown to over 1.5 million pet parents who rely on their guidance, seeking to maximize the time they have with their cherished animal companions.

# INDEX